Human
Rights:
A Contemporary Discussion

Dr. Shyam S. Khinchi

RIGI PUBLICATION

All right reserved

Human Rights:
A Contemporary Discussion

BY

Dr. Shyam S. Khinchi

Originally published in India

ISBN: 978-93-88393-43-0 (Paperback)

ISBN: 978-93-88393-44-7 (eBook)

Published by RIGI PUBLICATION

777, Street no.9, Krishna Nagar
Khanna-141401 (Punjab), India
Website: www.rigipublication.com
Email: info@rigipublication.com
Phone: +91-9357710014, +91-9465468291

DISCLAIMER

The findings/views/opinions expressed in this book are solely those of the authors and do not necessarily reflect the views of the editor.

CONTENTS

PREFACE

In the book I tried intensively to revealed all the basic rights and freedoms to which all humans are entitled.

Examples of rights and freedoms which are often thought of as human rights include civil and political rights, such as the right to life, liberty, property, freedom of expression, pursuit of happiness and equality before the law; and the social, cultural, economic rights, including the right to participate in science and culture, the right to work and education.

All human beings are born free and equal in dignity and rights. They are endowed with reason and conscience and should act towards one another in a spirit of brotherhood.

Dr. Shyam S. Khinchi

CHAPTER
1

HUMAN RIGHTS – MEANING AND CONCEPTS

Dr. Mohan Lal Goswami
Assistant Professor
Department of Political Science
SNDB Govt. P.G. College,
Nohar-Hanumangarh
(Rajasthan)

Introduction

Gandhi has been attributed as being the inspiration or model for various rights struggles around the world. In seeking to understand the notion of human rights in the context of the approach and ideology of Mahatma Gandhi, let us examine the notion of human rights. What are human rights? Are they moral rights, or are they legal rights? Then we focus on the Indian context, sketching the views of Gandhi, and contrasting these with those of Ambedkar, his arch-rival and the architect of the Indian constitution

The Concept of Human Rights

The term "human rights" has been made familiar by its use in today's international political discourse, and the prominence accorded to it by the media. However, its meaning is not always apparent or indisputable. Without going into abstract philosophical debates, it would suffice to say that a right is something to which we are entitled. This word in ordinary English usage not only means a "lawful entitlement"; it also means a "just entitlement."[1]"Human rights" is an even more complex term. The idea of human rights or the rights of the individual is commonly associated with the various forms of liberal individualism as they developed in the West.

The human rights movement, as we know it today, began in order to check state violation of constitutional rights or norms and make the state more accountable. More specifically, it is the result of the experiences of the Second World War. There seems to be international political consensus on the list of rights in Universal Declaration of Human Rights, which is explicitly endorsed by all nations. However, there is a lack of consensus among philosophers, political scientists, and rights scholars on the philosophy, origins, or justifications of the ideas of human rights. Other questions that occupy them relate to the universality of human rights and to the status of social, economic, and cultural rights.[2]While most authors believe that human rights are vital, they disagree about the nature and source of authority of human rights. They argue that without a legal status, rights cannot be enforced. In this debate it is important to note that where human rights are upheld by laws, they can be both moral as well as legal rights.In this very context, the question of the justification of human rights is perhaps more fundamental: How does being human give rise to rights? According to a moral or philosophical approach, human rights are necessary to human dignity.[3] Some of the sources of legitimacy identified are religion or morality modified by medieval philosophers, and later espoused by political thinkers who saw human rights as derived from the principles of the law of nature contending that human rights stem from a higher law than the state. The positivists, on the other hand, contend that all authority stems from what the state and officials have prescribed.[4] In the modern Indian context, Mohanty contends: Rights have been conceptualized not as claims recognized by the state but as political affirmations pursued through struggles. This is not to say that rights need no sanction of the state. It is to assert that even if they do not have the state sanction they are rights because they are accepted by the current stage of the human civilization as basic conditions deserved for every human being. The struggle for rights seeks state recognition but pursues it in society and culture to further realize it in practice.[5]

This is indeed how it was in the colonial period and in the 50 years after national independence.[6] But this way of looking at it brings human rights closer to the notion of natural or moral rights. Or, is it, in the Gandhian perspective, imposing a duty on the state to recognize the rights of the people? Gandhi's notion of human rights is closer to the views of the moralists. And interestingly, the view of Ambedkar, is that rights are positive rights.

Gandhi: The Moral Concept

What was Gandhi's ideology as far as human rights are

concerned? As the leader of the national freedom movement, Gandhi's objective was to attain independence, but his other objective was to save Indian society. He insisted that India should show her capacity to reform herself even while asking for freedom. His method of integrating nationalist aspirations within the framework of social reform explains his extraordinary tactics, for example, his manner of suddenly calling off a movement when the nature of the movement turned violent.[7]An important aspect of Gandhi's reform was that it had to take place absolutely within Hinduism. This was illustrated in Poona in 1931 when he fasted to exact from Ambedkar his withdrawal of the demand of a separate electorate for the Untouchables.[8]His thrust was that of a social reformer campaigning amongst the higher castes of the Hindu community, propagating social acceptance of the Untouchables by the community. In this process, he renamed the Untouchables "Harijans" (sons of God).Gandhi's programme of social reform was based on duties rather than on rights. He said very clearly that he did not care for rights, but for duties:If all simply insist on rights and no duties, there will be utter confusion and chaos. If instead of insisting on rights everyone dies his duty, there will immediately be the rule of order established among manking.[9] Not only did he value duties more than rights, but went further to say that the assertion of rights might even be harmful:While it is true that...hereditary inequalities must go as being injurious to the well-being of society, the unabashed assertion of rights of the hitherto downtrodden millions us equally injurious, if not more so, to the same well-being. The latter behavior is probably calculated to injure the millions rather than the few claimants of divine or other rights. They could not die a brave or cowardly death but those few dead would not bring in the orderly life of blissful contenetment.[10] He argued that if there were any rights at all, it could only be the result of well-performed duties: It is therefore necessary to understand the correlation between rights and duties. I venture to suggest that rights that do not flow directly from duty well-performed are not worth having. They will be usurpations sooner discarded the better.[11] When someone does not perform his duty in relation to someone else, Gandhi takes the example of the prince and the ryot (peasant). He says that if princes, whose duty is to act servants of the people, fail to perform their duty, "the ryots not only owe no return duty, but the duty devolves on them of resisting the princely usurpation. It may be otherwise said that ryots earn the right to resisting the usurpation or misrule." This resistance must, however, be peaceful, in keeping with the doctrine of ahimsa (nonviolence): "The resistance will become a crime against man in terms of duty if it takes the form of murder, rapine, and plunder."[12] When H.G. Wells[13] sought Gandhi's opinion on the "Rights of Man" drawn up by him, Gandhi argued for a "Charter of Duties" instead. The text of the cable that Gandhi sent to Wells sets out his views regarding rights and duties in no uncertain terms.[14] Received your cable. Have carefully read your five articles. You will permit me to say that you are in the wrong track. I feel sure that I can draw up a better charter of rights than you have drawn up. But what good will it be? Who will become its guardian? If you mean propaganda or popular education, you have begun at the wrong end. I suggest the right way. Begin with a charter of Duties of Man (both M and D capitals) and I promise the rights will follow as spring follows winter. I write from experience. As a young man I began life by seeking to assert my rights and I soon discovered I had none, not even over my wife. So I began by discovering and performing my duty by my wife, my children, friends, companions, and society and I find today that I have greater rights perhaps than any living man I know. If this too tall a claim, then I say I do not know anyone who possesses greater rights than I.Gandhi takes the attitude of a social reformer calling upon the higher castes to accept the Untouchables. He does not say that the Untouchables have rights, but says that upper castes have a duty towards them. When he advocates resistance, he adds that it must be done in the manner of Satyagraha—that is, not by asking for rights, but by showing the other person what his duty is. It is obvious that Gandhian notions are not sympathetic to human rights unless they are products of duties well-performed

Ambedkar: The Legal Concept

Gandhi's views can be contrasted with those of Ambedkar (1892-1956). Though both championed the cause of the Untouchables, their approaches differed widely.The Untouchables were designated as Scheduled Castes under the Government of India Act of 1935—and this term is still in use. Gandhi had started and popularized the term Harijan for the Untouchables (though many saw it as patronizing). Ambedkar, however, continued to use the term Untouchables.[15] The term now being increasingly used for them is "dalit" denoting "the oppressed."[16]Ambedkar characterized the national movement led by Gandhi as the "struggle for power distinguished from freedom" and accused all political parties of showing no concern for the cause of the Untouchables. He firmly believed that the caste Hindus would not concede any rights to the Untouchables due to the very nature of Hinduism itself: "The Hindus have an innate and inveterate conservatism and they have a religion which is incompatible with liberty, equality, and fraternity, i.e. with democracy."[17] It might be said that he simply did not trust theHindus.His position thus led him to assert that the Hindus and Untouchables were "not merely different by antagonistic," and demand that the Untouchables ought to be treated as:

Conclusion

The wider concept of claims is still the starting point for the understanding of the term "rights." Those claims which are in accordance of with some objective standards, whether those of a code of morality or those of a legal system—are usually and aptly called rights. Depending on the basis of recognition, they may be called moral or legal rights.[21] Thus rights which are laid down in law are called legal rights. They may be defended in a national court of law. Rights arising out of general principles of fairness and justice are called moral rights. A moral right may or may not be supported by the law of the land. Moral rights are thus claimed by "people in particular situations." They are not rights that can be claimed by all people in all situation.[22]In spite of theoretical debates, any movement for social or political reform which claims to be promoting freedom in some form or other (social justice, social transformation, etc.) is guaranteed a measure of respect. Few among us would want to be identified as hostile to freedom of human rights. Rights organizations play a significant role in promoting and protecting the rights of individuals and groups, often mediating between them and the state. A large number of rights organizations in India see questions of human rights as necessarily having a moral slant; but as they seek solutions to various kinds of abuses, they are often forced to recognize the paramount importance of the role of governmental agencies. To accept Gandhi's notion that rights and duties are two sides of the same coin would be too simplistic. It can be valid only in an ideal world, but since we live in the grim reality of humans fighting not only for resources, but for self-respect and dignity, the notion of rights assumes added significance. The notion of duties has sadly been used by those in position of power either to deny rights to others, or to dole out peaceful favours, eroding not only the dignity of the recipients of such so-called favours, but also eroding the power of the others to work towards standing on their own feet.Though Gandhi did not agree to becoming a part of Nehru's civil liberties organization, he nonetheless has become a symbol for rights organizations all over the world. Similarly, Ambedkar is a symbol of dalit identity, inspiring several social and political movements with a view to restoring dignity to the so-called lower castes. Zelliot has aptly summarized the relative positions of Gandhi and Ambedkar.Gandhi sought to change the heart of the caste Hindus by moral pressure within the framework of Hindu tradition. Ambedkar continued to work in the fields of education and politics in an attempt to gain legal rights for the Untouchables in the secular world.[23]Ambedkar's methods and solutions for the advancement of Untouchables, through legal and constitutional measures seems more in tune with the realities of Indian social order than Gandhi's attempt "to change the caste Hindus." It is not surprising, therefore, that the guiding ideology of the Untouchables, scheduled castes, and other backward castes in modern India is that of Ambedkar rather than that of Gandhi. It is also amply clear that the final aim of both the leaders was the same—to achieve some kind of equality among different strata of people, to end exploitation, and to ensure a life of dignity for all.

Both the leaders have thus in their own ways been responsible for the establishment and ideological sustenance of a large number of organizations that claim to work in the field of human rights.

References

1. Selby, David. 1987. *Human Rights*. Cambridge University Press, Cambridge. pp.7.

2. Donnelly, Jack. 1993. *International Human Rights*. X, West View Press, Cambridge. pp. 25.

3. Donnelly, Jack Donnelly, *International Human Rights*, pp. 21.

4. Shestack, Jerome, J. 1984. "The Jurisprudence of Human Rights," in Theodor Meron, ed., *Human Rights in International Law: Legal and Policy Issues.* Clarendon Press, Oxford. Vol.1, pp.75-83.

5. Mohanty, Manoranjan. 2002. "The Changing Definition of Rights in India," in Sujata Patel, Jasodhara Bagchi, and Krishna Raj, (eds.), *Thinking Social Sciences in India: Essays in Honour of Alice Thorner.* Sage, New Delhi. pp.437.

6. For a brief account of the establishment of the first human rights organizations in India, see Munmum Jha, "Nehru and Civil Liberties in India," in *International Journal of Human Rights*, Volume 7, Number 3, pp.103-115

7. An excellent example is calling of the Non Co-operation movement in February 1922 after a crowd attacked a police station in Chauri Chaura, killing 22 policemen. See A.R. *Social Background of Indian Nationalism* (Bombay: Popular Prakashan, 1976) pp. 352

8. Dumont, Louis.1970. "Nationalism and Communalism," in *Religion, Politics and History in India: Collected Papers in Indian Sociology*. Mouton Publishers, Paris.pp.104.

9. Gandhi, M. K. "Rights and Duties," in Raghvan Iyer, ed., *The Moral and Political Writings of Mahatma*

10. *Gandhi* (Oxford: Clarendon Press, 1986), Vol. 3, p. 496. (First published in Harijan, 6 July 1947).

11. *Ibid*.

12. *Ibid*.

13. *Ibid*., p. 498.

14. George, Wells Herbert. (1886-1946). English Novelist and Historian; author of *The Time Machine, The War of the Worlds, The Shape of Things to Come, The Outline of History, The Invisible Man,* and various other works.

15. Gandhi as quoted in Raghvan Iyer, *The Moral and Political Writings of Mahatma Gandhi*, Vol. 3, p. 492-3. (First published in The Hindustan Times, 16 April 1940).

16. Ambedkar, B. R. *Emancipation of the Untouchables* (Bombay: Thacker and Co. Ltd., 1972),pp.15. (First

published in 1943). For a discussion of various terms for the Untouchables, see Harold R. Isaacs, "The Ex-Untouchables," in Michael J. Mahar, ed., *The Untouchables in Contemporary India*, pp. 13-14

17. The term "Dalit" popularized by the protest movements since the 1970s, includes all backward sections, and at times, specifically the Untouchables. See Barbara R.Joshi, ed., *Untouchable! Voices of the Dalit Liberation Movement* (London: Zed Books and The Minority Rights Group, 1986), pp. 3-4

18. Ambedkar, B. R. *Emancipation of the Untouchables*, pp. 52-53.

19. *Ibid.*, pp. 15-18, 32-33, 37 and 40.

20. *Ibid.*, pp. 16 and 31

21. *Ibid.*, pp. 15-16 and 24-30

22. Dowrick, F.E. ed., *Human Rights: Problems, Perspectives and Texts*, (Aldershot: Gower), p.8.

23. Selby, David. *Human Rights*, pp. 6-8; see also Maurice Cranston, *What Are Human Rights*? P. 19-22

24. Zelliot, Eleanor "Gandhi and Ambedkar—A Study in Leadership," p.86

CHAPTER 2

HUMAN RIGHTS-SOME ASPECTS OF ITS HISTORY: AN EVOLUTION

Domitel D'Souza
Associate Professor
Department of History
Shree Mallikarjun College,
Canacona-GOA.

Introduction

The basic premises of understanding when we debate on the issue of human rights is that humans have not been gifted with the rights by law or the State but these rights were inherent in man by the very virtue of being born on this earth as humans. The Law only states or reiterates the rights of man which they already have. Morality and the virtues of being human were the guarantee that man would enjoy these rights and would allow other man to enjoy his rights. But unfortunately since the origin of human and society the story of man's discrimination, atrocities and struggle with his rights began. The law of the jungle, the *'matsyanyaya'* in Indian terminology or the 'survival of the fittest' took order of the day. History is replete with stories of horror, violation of basic rights, from the very beginning of times. The earliest account of the violation is Cain's murder of his brother Abel accounted for in the Old Testament of the Jewish tradition, where the right to life or living was violated; slavery in Greece and later in America and Abraham Lincoln championing the rights of the slaves to freedom, the account of horror of the Nazi Holocaust, or the World War I and II situation where the rights of the other States were infringed upon are all accounts of human rights violation. The war situation led to destruction of life, property, causing misery and infringement on the human right to live and enjoy a life of peace.

Let's be explicit with what these human rights imply. Human rights are rightsinherent to all human beings by virtue of their birth as human irrespective of colour, religion, origin or place of birth. An uncomplicated understanding of the term Human rights is those rights; to which all human beings are entitled to simply because of the fact that he/she is humans. These are fundamental and inalienable rights essential for life to be lived as human beings. These rights are inherent and one cannot live as human without them. These rights help a person to attain his highest self as a human and live a life of dignity. They are called as fundamental, basic or natural rights, or also as 'common rights'.

These rights are expressed and guaranteed by law. They are

characterized by being inherent, inalienable and equally applicable. Human rights are preconditions for human development. The individual has relation with the State and also amongst his fellow citizens. The individual- State relation is called 'vertical effect' of human rights. Several of these rights can have implication for relations among individuals which is called 'horizontal effect.'This implies that the government has an important role to play; it should refrain from violating human rights of its citizens but also has the duty to protect the individual from infringement upon his rights by others and also prevent him from infringing upon the rights of the other individuals.

Various theories have been expounded to explain these rights

1. Natural Law Theory: The credit for expounding this theory goes to the Greek scholars Sophocles and Aristotle. The Romans law 'Jus Civil' and 'Jus Gentium' were categorized as natural laws. These rights are seen as in the very nature of man or the law of nature and are eternal. John Locke was an exponent of this law. He stated man is in his natural state of freedom and equality.

2. Positivism/ Authority of the State: The advocates of this theory believe in the State as maker of law and upholder of these rights. So law gains primacy.The People are bound to obey the law if created by appropriate legislative authority.

3. Marxist Theory: The Marxist saw individual rights as synonymous with the rights of society. The upliftment of the society or community is seen as primary for the higher freedoms of individuals to be achieved.

4. Theories Based on Justice: Justice is seen as a primary virtue of social institution. Through the principle of justice, rights and duties are assigned in the institution of society and also appropriate distribution of benefits and burdens of social cooperation. It is based on the principle of fairness.

5. Theories Based on Dignity: The advocate of this theory believe that protection of human dignity is the primary goal of any social policy. The goal should be to ensure a world community in which there is democratic distribution of values and the available resources are utilized to the maximum and protection of human dignity stands in primacy.

6. Theory Based on Equality of Respect and Concern: The advocates of these theory states that the government should treat its citizen with equal respect and concern which is the basis for this rights to be enjoyed by all.

The onus is on the government for protection of these rights and to ensure that these rights are not violated and enjoyed by all which is the basic principle of good governance. Law had to be envisaged to protect and ensure that all man enjoy these right and also prevention of violation of these rights. Though Human rights is said to be a western concept, all cultures had a consciousness of these rights and no culture would uphold brutalities, however the terminology came into existence much later. In every society there were advocates of these rights. The origin can be traced to 'divine theory' which stipulates that we are created equal by the divine, reminding of Jean Jacques Rousseau (1712-1778) the French thinker who stated 'Man is born free and everywhere he is in chains.'

The first Human right declaration is said to be Cyrus cylinder 539 B.C.E which is his clay tablet which declares certain basic rights to his subjects. Another exemplar for promulgation of the law is Hammurabi's code 1754 B.C.E., with the famous dictum 'an eye for an eye and tooth for a tooth.' This is considered as the first written law from ancient Mesopotamia. Though it is harsh in nature, it did advocate the protection of the right of man and harsh punishment for violating the right. The Greeks seem to have given a greater meaning to these rights. Socrates and Plato defined natural rights and natural laws as synonymous. Aristotle the Greek Philosopher had a conception of rights and believed that the constitution would assign rights to its citizens. The Roman law 'Jus Civil' and 'Jus Gentium'(law of citizens and law of non citizens) is said to be a link between the classical Greek thought and modern conception.

The Magna Carta of 1215 could be claimed as precursor of modern conception of human rights. The Humanist (1400-1650) popularized the concept of rights. Thomas Paine was another advocate of rights of man, he advocated American Independence through his 'Commonsense' in (1776). Edmund Burke (served as a member of the British parliament with Whig Party 1766-1994) subscribed to natural law theory while Jeremy Bentham (1748-1832 English philosopher a utilitarian) advocated law and legal rights. Earlier Thomas Hobbes (1588-1679) in England drew distinction between rights and law. He argued thatright was liberty and law was restrain so right and law not only differed from each other but was also opposite. There is a view that the modern conception of human rights is derived from Locke's Second Treatise of government. John Locke was a Scottish philosopher lived between 1632-1704.The American Declaration of Independence (1776) drafted by Thomas Jefferson expressed Locke's ideas. First defined by The 'Virginia Declaration of Rights' in June1776 which preceded the American declaration is best expression is proclaims all men are by nature equally free and independent and have certain inherent rights... The 1791 Bill of Rights authored by James Madison also speaks of certain rights and freedom.

The great revolutions were a struggle for rights and the desire to bring a new world order. The American Revolution stood for democratic value and completed with the framing of the democratic constitution. The French revolution of 1789 fought against the social and economic inequality and injustice of the French Emperor and the National Assembly prepared the 'Declaration of Rights of Man' a crucial document on Human rights an example for the word struggling for Human rights. The French gave to the world the ideals of liberty, fraternity and equality. The Russian Revolution stood for social and economic justice.

Though Human rights are a modern conceptualization it has its roots in the very past. One paradigm states that the concept of Human Rights could be found in the religions and philosophies of the world. Others would state it originated in the west. It is argued that non western cultures had ethical concepts but not the concept of Human rights. Individual having rights against the state was unthinkable in the past.

The horror of the world wars brought a realization of the

necessity of peace so the world witnessed the emergence of the League of Nation after the World War I and the historic United Nation Organization (UNO) entrusted with the task of maintaining world peace and prevention of disaster. The term Human rights is said to emerge in 1945 after the end of World War II. It has been stated that the concept of Human Rights begins with the establishment of United Nations in1945. The concept of UN is associated with Human Rights. It is a common standard of achievement for all people and all nations'

United Nations Declaration of Human Rights was adopted on 10th Dec. 1948. Thereafter there were two conventions adopted thereafter by United Nations in 1960 'The International Convention on civil and political rights' and 'International convention on Economic social and cultural rights'. Human Rights were classified by UN into five categories- Civil, Political, Economic, Social and Cultural. With the Universal Declaration on Human Rights, Human Rights became a matter of international concern. An effort was made to regulate Human Rights at international level. However Human Rights need not be a document but a thought which can change the ruling on Human Rights.

India accepted the UN Declaration of Human Rights on 10th Dec, 1948. The struggle for India's independence was also a movement for human right- i.e. attainment of freedom. As B. G. Tilak the Indian nationalist stated 'freedom is my birthright'. India did get freedom from imperialism in 1947 but the socio-economic freedom was still evasive. The struggle had to continue. The Indian Constitution was adopted in 1950. Part III of the Constitution guarantees to its citizens an array of Fundamental Rights and Art 51A

Fundamental Duties likewise. Apart from it there are a number of legislation on every form of violation of rights.

Way before the Constitution was adoptedwhich ensured that the citizens enjoy a life of dignity, the socio-religious reformers in India did attempt to provide the downtrodden with a life of dignity by attempting to do away with the religious dogmas and superstitions, by doing away with the social evils like child marriage untouchability and women related harrow like sati. Raja Ram Mohan Roy was considered as the herald of modern India, also were the likes of Swami Vivekanand, Jyotiba Phule, Dayanand Saraswati and many others social reformers of India.India also has an example of the Great Emperor Ashoka who gave up war to ensure peace and dignified life to his subjects and nations around. Human rights Act was enacted in 1993 which defined human rights as relating to liberty equality and dignity of individuals guaranteed by the Indian constitution as embodied in the Fundamental rights and international covenants.

It is a reflection whether the generation of thinkers debating on the issue of Human rights and the laws enacted, has they been credited by the eradication of human rights violation or even lessen the instances of violation? Does our world of today uphold human dignity and the law ensures that man enjoys his rights fully? No amount of law can ensure a world safe and free from man who has become ethic- neutral and dehumanized. Mans morality and principle for which a man is defined as different from animals should be the guiding force for man, and a restrain on him infringing on the rights of others. Man as a Moral and rational beings respecting him and rights of others can ensure a world with a difference. The world today is replete with issues of human right violation, the violation of rights of women and children, migrants and refugees, terrorism and human trafficking on a scale unheard of before. Thus a debate on these issues needs to be ensued so as to ensure man living in freedom and without fear.In creating a noble feeling of universal brotherhood, the sustenance of human beings living a dignified life can be ensured. The world today has the ideals set by Abraham Lincoln, M. K. Gandhi, Nelson Mandela and many others who stands as a shining stars in field of human rights arena.

References

1. Freeman, M. 1988. Human Rights. Blackwell Publishers Inc. USA.

2. Kapoor, D. S. 2014. Human Rights. Central Law Agency, Allahabad.

3. Reichert, E. 2003. Social Work and Human Rights. Rawat Publication, Jaipur.

4. Samantroy, D. 2013.Handbook of Human Rights and Social Justice. Astha Publishers, New Delhi.

5. Saxena, K. 1999. Human Rights Fifty Years of India's Independenc. Gyan Publishing House, New Delhi.

6. Soni, S. K. 2007. Human Rights Concept. Issues. Emerging Problems. Regal Publication, New Delhi.

7. Wakman, P. K. 2013. Human Rights. Trinity Publishers, Karnataka.

CHAPTER 3

VIOLATION OF HUMAN RIGHTS IN INDIA – DISCRIMINATION BETWEEN THEORETICAL KNOWLEDGE & PRACTICAL IMPLEMENTATION

Sanat Kumar Purkait
Assistant Professor
Department of Geography,
Raidighi College,
(University of Calcutta)
South 24 Paraganas.
(West Bangal)

Introduction

From the very dawn of the civilization, it is found that the weaker section is dominated by the stronger one of the society. In the ancient period, the master of the society frames the rules and regulations of the society and if the said rules are gone through thoroughly with proper explanation, it will be clear that most of the rules are to dominate the downtrodden of the society. The upper class always exercised those rules on the poor and weaker section just by the name of religion. However, those cultures, rituals, religions and practices are modified from time to time for the benefit of the upper section. Sometimes, those are modified, better to say rectified by the social human being by a mass movement by the weaker section of the society. Actually, in course of time they became masters of the society with the help of those rules. Since the very early days of the Indus Valley Civilization, Indian culture has been the product of a synthesis of diverse cultures and religions that came into contact with the enormous Indian sub continent over a very long stretch of time. According to Pt. Jawaharlal Nehru, there is "an unbroken continuity between the most modern and the most ancient phases of Hindu thought extending over three thousand years".

The rights of man have been the concern of all civilizations from time immemorial. "The concept of the rights of man and other fundamental rights was not unknown to the people of earlier periods. "History says that the Babylonian Laws and the Assyrian laws in the Middle East, the "Dharma" of the Vedic period in India and the jurisprudence of Lao-Tze and Confucius in China, have championed human rights throughout the history of human civilization. Whereas, the Indian concept perceives the individual, the society and the universe as an organic whole, everyone is a child of God and all fellow beings are related to one another and belong to a universal family. In this context, Mahatma Gandhi remarks, "I do not want to think in terms of the whole world. My patriotism includes the good of mankind in general. Therefore my service to India includes the services of humanity."

Definition

Human rights are the basic rights and freedoms that belong to every person in the world, from birth until death. They apply regardless of where you are from, what you believe or how you choose to live your life. There are various contemporary definitions of human rights.

The **NHRC** is the National Human Rights Commission of India is responsible for the protection and promotion of human rights. According to the NHRC, the human rights may be defined by the Act as "..... rights relating to **life**, **liberty**, **equality** and **dignity** of the individual guaranteed by the **Constitution** or embodied in the **International Covenants**".

On the other hand, some social scientists opined that Human rights refer to the basic rights that are believed to be entitled to every human-being. Every human-being are entitled to certain rights and freedom irrespective of their origin, ethnicity, race, colour, nationality, citizenship, sex or religion. These rights are considered universal for humanity. They can never be taken away, although they can sometimes be restricted – for example if a person breaks the law, or in the interests of national security.

These basic rights are based on shared values like dignity, fairness, equality, respect and independence. These values are defined and protected by law. In Britain our human rights are protected by the Human Rights Act 1998.

The term 'Human Rights' is a dynamic concept. These rights may be called the basic rights, the fundamental rights as stated in the Indian Constitution, the natural rights or the inherent rights. The principal objective of both Indian and international laws is to protect the human personality and its fundamental rights.

According to the Business Dictionary, The fundamental rights are the rights that humans have by the fact of being human, and that are neither created nor can be abrogated by any government. Supported by several international conventions and treaties (such as the United Nation's Universal Declaration of Human rights in 1948), these include cultural, economic, and political rights, such as right to life, liberty, education and equality before law, and right of association, belief, free speech, information, religion, movement, and nationality. Promulgation of these rights is not binding on any country, but they serve as a standard of concern for people and form the basis of many modern national constitutions.

Although they were defined first by the Scottish philosopher John Locke (1632-1704) as absolute moral claims or entitlements to life, liberty, and property, the best-known expression of human rights is in the Virginia Declaration of Rights in 1776 which proclaims that "All men are by nature equally free and independent and have certain inherent rights, of which, when they enter a state of society, they cannot, by any compact, deprive or divest their posterity." It is called also fundamental rights.

According to United Nations Human Rights Office of the High Commissioner, Human rights are rights inherent to all human beings, whatever our nationality, place of residence, sex, national or ethnic origin, colour, religion, language, or any other status. We are all equally entitled to our human rights without discrimination. These rights are all interrelated, interdependent and indivisible.

Origin and Development of Human Rights in India

If we peep into the history back of the different parts of the world, we will find that every time is governed by a supreme religion, culture and different practices associated with the dominated religion. When the people are deprived by the society, they follow the doctrine as proposed by their God or his followers. Just like The Buddhist doctrine of non-violence in deed, "is a humanitarian doctrine par excellence, dating back to the third century B.C." His doctrines of peace, his Astangik Marg (Eight Enlighten Paths) are the main source to relief the poor people from the junk of their daily life. In that way, Jainism too contained similar doctrines. In the belief of Hinduism according to the Shrimad Bhagbad Gita, *"he who has no ill will to any being, who is friendly and compassionate, who is free from egoism and self sense and who is even-minded in pain and pleasure and patient"* is dear to God. When the society is busy with violence and the honest people were deprived by the naughty one, the God Krishna advised Arjuna to resolve the contemporary problems of their daily life. In this way, he wants to provide the rights of the deprived people who really deserve that. It also says that divinity in humans is represented by the virtues of non-violence, truth, freedom from anger, renunciation, aversion to fault-finding, compassion to living being; freedom from covetousness, gentleness, modesty and steadiness -the qualities that a good human being ought to have. The historical account of ancient Bharat proves beyond doubt that human rights were as muck manifest in the ancient Hindu and Islamic civilizations as in the European Christian civilizations. The Ashoka, the prophet Mohammed and Great

Mughal emperor Akbar cannot be excluded from the genealogy of human rights.

Ancient Hindu Law of Human Rights

Scholars who have spent long time in lucubration on the Hindu "Dharmasastras" and the "Arthasastras" and other legal treatises of the past have discovered an amazing system, which, interalia, regulates the duties of Kings, judges, subjects and judicial as well as legal procedures. The central concept is Dharma, the functional focus of which is social order. The message is "Dharma" as the supreme value, which binds kings and citizens, men and women. Human rights gain meaning only when there is an independent judiciary to enforce rights. Here, the Dharmasastras are clear and categoric.

The independence of the judiciary was one of the outstanding features of the Hindu judicial system. Even during the days of Hindu monarchy, the administration of justice always remained separate from the executive. It was, as a rule, independent both in form and spirit. It was the Hindu judicial system that first realized and recognized the importance of the separation of the judiciary from the executive and gave this fundamental principle a practical shape and form. The case of *Ananthapindika* v. *Jeta* reported in the *vinaya-pitaka,'* is a shining illustration of this principle. According to it, a Prince and a private citizen submitted their cases before the law court arid the court decided against the Prince. The Prince accepted the decision as a matter of course and as binding on him. The evolution f the principle of separation of the judiciary from the executive was largely the result of the Hindu conception of law as binding on the sovereign. Law in Hindu jurisprudence was above the sovereign. It was the "Dharma."

The laws were then not regarded so much as a product of supreme Parliaments and Legislatures as at present. Certain laws were regarded as above all human authority. Such, for instance, were the natural laws, which no Parliament, however supreme, could abolish. "The State was not sacerdotal, nor even paternalistic; even the King as subject to the law, as any other citizen and the 'Divine Right' of Kings known to western political science was unknown to India. On the whole, the aim of the ancient Indian State may be said to have been less to introduce an improved social order, than to act in conformity with the established moral order." Duty is not a tyrant, but a symbol of dignity to be discharged with affirmative joy. The realization of this vast perspective is assured in the Dharmasastras by the wonderful scheme or co-ordination of conduct adapted to different conditions, status and situations of life. The scope of dharma takes in its vast sweep human rights as well.

If we go through the sloka of sikshastakam of Sri Sri Mahaprabhu Sri Chaitanya, one sloka *"Trinadapi Sunicheno Taroribo Sohisnuna, Amanina Manodeno Krtoniyo Sadahori"* depicts that the equal honour should be offered to the all levels of people. Mahaprabhu wrote this sloka to eradicate this difference between Brahman, the upper class and the Sudra, the lower class of the society.

United Nations Universal Declaration of Human Rights

The Universal Declaration of Human Rights (UDHR) is a milestone document in the history of human rights. Drafted by representatives with different legal and cultural backgrounds from all regions of the world, the Declaration was proclaimed by the United Nations General Assembly in Paris on 10 December 1948 (General Assembly resolution 217 A) as a common standard of achievements for all peoples and all nations. It sets out, for the first time, fundamental human rights to be universally protected and it has been translated into over 500 languages.

Article 1 Equality to Religion & Conscience: All human beings are born free and equal in dignity and rights. They are endowed with *religion* and conscience and should act towards one another in a spirit of brotherhood.

Article 2 Equal Rights & Freedoms: Everyone is entitled to all the rights and freedoms set forth in this Declaration, without distinction of any kind, such as race, color, sex, language, religion, political or other opinion, national or social origin, property, birth or other status. Furthermore, no distinction shall be made on the basis of the political, jurisdictional or international status of the country or territory to which a person belongs, whether it is independent, trust, non-self-governing or under any other limitation of sovereignty.

Article 3 Right to Personal Liberty in life: Everyone has the right to life, liberty and security of person.

Article 4 Slavery & Forced Labour: No one shall be held in slavery or servitude; slavery and the slave trade shall be prohibited in all their forms.

Article 5 Protection from Prosecution and Punishment: No one shall be subjected to torture or to cruel, inhuman or degrading treatment or punishment.

Article 6 Right to Recognition: Everyone has the right to recognition everywhere as a person before the law.

Article 7 Equality before Law: All are equal before the law and are entitled without any discrimination to equal protection of the law. All are entitled to equal protection against any discrimination in violation of this Declaration and against any incitement to such discrimination.

Article 8 Right to Constitutional rights: Everyone has the right to an effective remedy by the competent national tribunals for acts violating the fundamental rights granted him by the constitution or by law.

Article 9 Protection against Arrest and detention: No one shall be subjected to arbitrary arrest, detention or exile.

Article 10 Right to have the Judgement: Everyone is entitled in full equality to a fair and public hearing by an independent and impartial tribunal, in the determination of his rights and obligations and of any criminal charge against him.

Article 11 Right to self Defense:

(1) Everyone charged with a penal offence has the right to be presumed innocent until proved guilty according to law in a public trial at which he has had all the guarantees necessary for his defense.

(2) No one shall be held guilty of any penal offence on account of any act or omission which did not constitute a penal offence, under national or international law, at the time when it was committed. Nor shall a heavier penalty be imposed than the one that was applicable at the time the penal offence was committed.

Article 12 Protection from Personal Attacks: No one shall be subjected to arbitrary interference with his privacy, family, home or correspondence, or to attacks upon his honour and reputation. Everyone has the right to the protection of the law against such interference or attacks.

Article 13 Right to Free Movement within the border of the State:

(1) Everyone has the right to freedom of movement and residence within the borders of each state.

(2) Everyone has the right to leave any country, including his own, and to return to his country.

Article 14 Protection from Crime:

(1) Everyone has the right to seek and to enjoy in other countries asylum from persecution.

(2) This right may not be invoked in the case of prosecutions genuinely arising from non-political crimes or from acts contrary to the purposes and principles of the United Nations.

Article 15 Right to National Identity:

(1) Everyone has the right to a nationality. (2) No one shall be arbitrarily deprived of his nationality nor denied the right to change his nationality.

Article 16 Marriage and Family: Every grown-up has the right to marry and have a family if they want to. Men and women have the same rights when they are married, and when they are separated.

(1) Men and women of full age, without any limitation due to race, nationality or religion, have the right to marry and to found a family. They are entitled to equal rights as to marriage, during marriage and at its dissolution.

(2) Marriage shall be entered into only with the free and full consent of the intending spouses.

(3) The family is the natural and fundamental group unit of society and is entitled to protection by society and the State.

Article 17 The Right to Your Own Things: Everyone has the right to own things or share them. Nobody should take our things from us without a good reason.

Article 18 Freedom of Thought: We all have the right to believe in what we want to believe, to have a religion, or to change it if we want.

Article 19 Freedom of Expression: We all have the right to make up our own minds, to think what we like, to say what we think, and to share our ideas with other people.

Article 20 The Right to Public Assembly: We all have the right to meet our friends and to work together in peace to defend our rights. Nobody can make us join a group if we don't want to.

Article 21 The Right to Democracy: We all have the right to take part in the government of our country. Every grown-up should be allowed to choose their own leaders.

Article 22 Social Security: We all have the right to affordable housing, medicine, education, and childcare, enough money to live on and medical help if we are ill or old.

Article 23 Workers' Rights: Every grown-up has the right to do a job, to a fair wage for their work, and to join a trade union.

Article 24 Right to Play: We all have the right to rest from work and to relax.

Article 25 Food and Shelter for All: We all have the right to a good life. Mothers and children, people who are old, unemployed or disabled, and all people have the right to be cared for.

Article 26 The Right to Education: Education is a right. Primary school should be free. We should learn about the United Nations and how to get on with others. Our parents can choose what we learn.

Article 27 Copyright: Copyright is a special law that protects one's own artistic creations and writings; others cannot make copies without permission. We all have the right to our own way of life and to enjoy the good things that art, science and learning bring.

Article 28 Right to A Fair and Free World: There must be proper order so we can all enjoy rights and freedoms in our own country and all over the world.

Article 29 Responsibility: We have a duty to other people, and we should protect their rights and freedoms.

Article 30 No One Can Take Away Your Human Rights.

Human Rights in India

Human rights in India require the existence and protection of a well regulated society. Only the society and the state can guarantee these human rights to the individual. But to enjoy the rights perfectly the citizens of India too much observe the social norms properly.

India has also enacted the protection of Human rights Act in 1993 and also constituted the National Human Rights Commission, the State Human Rights Commission in different States and Human Right Courts. In spite of these apparently fixed positions, some shifts are also visible in each perspective of human rights. Violation of human rights in India is now seen as violations of the democratic principles enshrined in the Indian Constitution as well as violation of India's international commitment of humanitarian international law and international covenants. We can make a comparative study of Different Articles of the Universal Declaration of Human Rights on Civil and Political Rights and the Rights assured by the Indian Constitution *(See Table No.1)*

Table1 1: Comparative Study of Different Articles of the Universal Declaration of Human Rights on Civil and Political Rights and the Indian Constitution

Sr. No	Fundamental Rights	Universal Declaration	Indian Constitution
1	Equality before Law	Article 7	Article 14
2	Prohibition of Discrimination	Article 7	Article 15(1)

3	Equality of opportunity to Public Service	Article 21(2)	Article 16(1)
4	Freedom of Speech and Expression	Article 19	Article 19(1a)
5	Right to peaceful assembly	Article 20(1)	Article 19(1b)
6	Right to Freedom of Association or Unions	Article 23(4)	Article 19(1c)
7	Right to move freely within the Border	Article 13(1)	Article 19(1d)
8	Protection in respect of conviction of offences	Article 11(2)	Article 20(1)
9	Right to Life and Personal Liberty	Article 3	Article 21
10	Protection of Slavery & Forced Labour	Article 4	Article 23
11	Freedom of Conscience and Religion	Article 18	Article 25(1)
12	Remedy for enforcement of rights	Article 8	Article 32
13	Right against arbitrary arrest and Detention	Article 9	Article 22
14	Right to Social Security	Article 22	Article 29(1)

Political Rights and Human Rights in India

India is the largest representative democracy in the world, based on universal adult suffrage, providing every Indian of at least eighteen years of age the right to vote. The Indian Constitution provides for direct elections to the House of the People of the Central Parliament, i.e. the Lok Sabha and the State: Provincial) Legislative Assemblies, once in every five years at the latest. The members of the State Legislatures dothe elections to the Council of States, i.e. Rajya Sabha, which is the upper house of Parliament. The elected members of Parliament and State Legislative Assemblies elect the President. Both the Houses of Parliament together elect the Vice-President. The right to vote, the right to contest elections, and the conduct of elections are all governed by the Constitution (Part XV) as well as special laws like the Representation of the People Act, 1951. The Constitution provides for an independent Election Commission (Article 324), which has in fact acquitted itself quite admirably in the recent elections, both provincial as well as parliamentary, and set an agenda for clean elections and elimination of the criminal politician nexus. We may look into the comparative study between International Covenant on Civil and Political Rights and the Indian Constitution (See Table: 2)

Table 2: Comparative Study of Different Articles of the International Covenant on Civil and Political Rights and the Indian Constitution

Sr. No	Fundamental Rights	Covenant on Civil & Political Rights	Indian Constitution
1	Forced Labour	Article 8(3)	Article 23
2	Equality before Law	Article 14(1)	Article 14
3	Prohibition of Discrimination	Article 26	Article 15
4	Equality of opportunity to Public Service	Article 25(C)	Article 16(1)
5	Freedom of Speech and Expression	Article 19 (1& 2)	Article 19(1a)
6	Right for peaceful assembly	Article 21	Article 19(1b)
7	Right to Freedom of Association	Article 22 (1)	Article 19(1c)
8	Right to move freely within the territory of a State	Article 12 (1)	Article 19(1d & e)
9	Protection in respect of conviction of offences	Article 15 (1)	Article 20(1)

10	Protection from prosecution and punishment	Article 14 (7)	Article 20(2)
11	Not to be compelled to testify against himself	Article 14 (3 g)	Article 20(3)
12	Right to Life and Liberty	Article 6(1) &9(1)	Article 21
13	Right to Child Education	Article 26(1)	Article 21(A)
14	Protection against Arrest and Detention	Article 9(2,3 &4)	Article 22
15	Freedom of Conscience and Religion	Article 18(1)	Article 25

Political Rights and Human Rights in Bengal

Now-a-days, it is the scenario of the Indian politics to snatch away all the political rights of the general people. The case study of Bengal says that in the latest Gram Panchayat General Election, the people of the opponent parties have no security at the time of issue of nomination and they who were very much interested to participate in this election as a candidate are assaulted and their family members are harassed in different sectors. Even, some of the murder cases including kidnapping cases have been registered in the local police stations of the districts of West Bengal. Apart from this, at the time of casting of their vote on their preference, they have no right to cast their own vote, because the ruling party does not belief in the voter's assurance. As a result, most of the booth and polling parties are the dumb witnesses of the booth capturing, open canvassing and ballot box snatching. But the State Government and the State Election Commission has no proper arrangement for the security of the general voter or for the polling personnel. One of the School teachers among the polling parties was kidnapped from the polling station and he was traced murdered. In fact, there is a gap between the human rights to political field and the implementation of the said rights among the mass. Most of the voters have returned from the booth without casting their own votes but unfortunately official records found that more than 90% votes were poled. It is the break of political rights among the mass people in Bengal.

Socio Economic Status and Human Rights in India

From the very outset of the civilization, our society especially the society belongs to the Hindu community is divided in many more frames. There you will find the division of four categories i.e. Brahman, Khatriya, Byasa and Sudra in accordance with their job pattern, rather it may be said that classification was based on the socio economic status o the people. The upper class started from the Brahman and ended with the Sudra. The Brahmans are regulator of the society and they are the supreme authority among the four class. Brahman will worship the God and frame the rules and regulation for the other three classes, the Kshatriya class will protect the Brahman, Byasa will be selected for the business and they are responsible for the feeding of the upper class and the lower stratum of this societal class will be designated as to service the upper three one. In course of time, there you will find the concept became modify. The people of those four classes are not necessarily busy with their scheduled sectors; rather they prefer those jobs from which maximum income may be generated. But, those characters of the upper class to dominate over the lower stratum are still in view.

At present, the categorizations of the people in accordance with the economic dependency are more relevant in contextual discussions of the implementations of human rights. There you will find General, SC, ST, OBC (Creamy & Non-Creamy Layer). From the very beginning of the independence, Baba Saheb Ambedkar, the father of Indian constitution carefully handled the case of the financially backwardness of the downtrodden people of the society. In constitution, there are certain sections assuring the reservation to provide economic support to assure right to education and reservation at the time recruitment. But, now-a-days, the general category, the creamy layer is in a position to tease the reserved categories and they are snatched the prestige and honour of their daily life by throwing the insulted words. So, implementation is very much crucial part to provide fundamental rights to the grass root level equally.

WOMEN HUMAN RIGHTS IN INDIA

There are many more human rights especially for the women in India by keeping the then miserable condition of the women in Indian society. They faced different malpractices of the society as determined by the master of the society i.e. furious Sati Practice, Prada Practice, historic Jauhar Practice and dangerous Devdasi system etc. In this paternal society, the women are frequently dominated by the male one throughout the historic era. The head of the family must be from the male one. In course of time, after the implementation of human rights with the independence of India the following rights in Indian Constitution are dedicated to the women that are much more than that of male. The fundamental human rights for the women in India are:

- Right to equality
- Right to education
- Right to liberty
- Right to get equal wages for equal work
- Right to protection from gender discrimination
- Right to social protection in the eventuality of retirement, old age and sickness
- Right to protection from inhuman treatment
- Right to politics
- Right to property
- Right to equal opportunity for employment
- Right to free choice of profession
- Right to livelihood
- Right to live with dignity
- Right to work in equitable condition
- Right to protection of health
- Right to privacy in terms of personal life, family, residence, correspondence etc.
- Right to protection from society, state and family system.

But, there are certain gaps between the theoretical explanation and practical implementation to the scenario of women human rights. Long long years passed, but the mentality of the society cannot be changed, even after getting the mass education among the people. The dominance of the male society is still now applicable to this society. It is much found among the tribal society or the dalit community. Even when the 50% seats in the assembly election are kept reserved for the women to assure the political rights, the women are merely a candidate, but her husband became the supreme authority for the said assembly. It is a matter of fact, the women are not safe and secure in the Indian society. That's why; it is completely troublesome to provide the women human rights fully. They are not free to move here and there without proper care and security, as a result, the dependency on male society triggers to the dominance of the male society on the female. Even Child marriage, Child Labour, Sex Workers, Dowry system are prevalent to the Indian society after the existence of the State Human Rights Commission.

Steps taken to protect Human Rights in India

In India, all citizens are entitled to enjoy the privilege of human rights. To protect the people to have the fundamental rights the govt. should take proper initiatives. Several initiatives have been undertaken in India for the greater protection of the women, children and certain other groups of the society such as:

1. The protection of Human Rights Act was enacted in 1993. In this act, the state is the guarantor to provide the environment regarding the equal enjoyment of the fundamental human rights.

2. The dangerous Sati Practices has been prohibited in India. Raja Rammohan Roy is the pioneer to eradicate this malpractice of the human society.

3. The minimum age for marriages has been fixed by law to

protect child marriage. A boy below the age of 21 and a girl below 18 years can not marry. Once in the ancient law of Hindu society, there is a provision of child marriage among the kulin Brahmin.

4. To protect the childhood, child labour especially below the age of 14 years is banned in factories and mines.

5. Right to education has been accepted as one of the fundamental rights in our country. In the year 2009, there the Free and Compulsory Education Act was passed to circulate the basic education among the children.

6. Dowry system has been prohibited by the law and Dowry Prohibition Act was passed in this regard in the year 1961. But, in some retarded area, this system is still alive among some of the tribal people or dalit community.

7. For the protection of women from domestic violence, Domestic violence Act was passed in 2005.

Conclusions

In this paper, there are many more fundamental rights assured by the Indian constitution, universal declarations of human rights assured by the United Nations and Covenant on Civil & Political Rights in the papers. Problems are laid down before the implementation of those rights among the general people equally. Law is not open to all the layers of the society. There is always a hierarchy in the subjects of human rights law. No human rights can be detracted from the individual's human rights and human rights laws recognize certain rights of the groups. Moreover, the diversity of the cultures and civilization, beliefs and traditions, history and aspirations reflected in politico legal system, give rise to ever changing meaning to human rights. So, there must be certain law and monitoring bodies to check the status of the utilization of the human rights. State Human Rights Commission, Central Human Rights Commission, High Court, Supreme Court should be proactive to monitor the societal gap among the different class.

Reference

1. Mafizul Islam Patwaris, A.B.M. 1991. *Fundamental Rights and Personal Liberty in India, Pakistan and Bangladesh*, 1ˢᵗ ed. Deep and Deep Publications, New Delhi. pp.63.

2. Chand, Attar. 1985. *Politics of Human Rights and Civil Liberties - A Global Survey*. UDH Publishers, Delhi. pp. 45.

3. *Crimes in India*. 2010, NCRB, Ministry of Home Affairs.

4. Susanne, Jalbert. E. 2000. *Women Entrepreneurs in the Global Economy*, March 17, 2000.

5. Nehru, Jawaharlal. 1992. *"The Discovery of India"*, 2nd ed. Jawaharlal Nehru Memorial Fund, New Delhi. pp.88.

6. Manohar, Justice Sujata V. 1996. *"Judiciary and Human Rights,"* Indian Journal of International Law. No. 2, Vol. 36, pp.45.

7. Singh, Nagendra. 1986. *Enforcement of Human Rights*. Eastern Law House Pvt. Ltd, Calcutta.

8. Jaswal, Paramjit S. and Jaswal, Nishtha.1995. *Human*

Rights and the Law, 1st ed. Ashish Publishing House, New Delhi.pp.5.

9.　Gadkar, P.B. Gajendra. 1965. The Historical Background and Theoretic Basis of Hindu Law - *The Cultural Heritage of India. Vol. II* (Asia Publishing House, Bombay. pp 421.

10.　Mukherji, P.B. 1999. The Hirldu Judicial System - The Cultural Heritage of India, Vol. II, 434-435. Cited by V.R. Krishna Iyer, *The Dialectics and Dynamics of Human Rights in India - Yesterday Today and Tomorrow, Tagore Law lectures*. Eastern Law House, Calcutta. pp. 115.

11.　Jois, Rama. 2001. Legal and constitutional History of India, Part-I. Universal Law Publishing Co. Ltd. New Delhi. pp. 13.

12.　Dhanua, Ritu. Violation of Women Human Rights in India. *Shiv Shakti International Journal in Multidisciplinary and Academic Research (SSIJMAR)* Vol. 1, No. 4, November-December (ISSN 2278 – 5973)

13.　Shashi. 2008. Indian Democracy and Women's Human Rights. *Madhya Pradesh Journal of Social Sciences.*

14.　Dhyani, S.N. 1992. Fundamentals of Jurisprudence: The Indian Approach. Central Law Agency, Allahabad.pp. 79.

15.　Radhakrishnan, S. 1958. (trans.) The Bhagavadgita. George Allen and Unwin, London. pp. 276.

16. Subramanian, S. 1997. *Human Rights. International Challenge*. Vol.1. Manas Publication, New Delhi.

17. Deshta, Sunil and Deshta, Kiran. 1995. "Philosophy of Right to Life, A Movement from Rigidity to Flexibility." *Civil and Military Law Journal,* Vol. 31:3. 123. (July-September.) pp. 101.

18. Krisha Iyer, R. 1999. The Dialectics and Dynamics of Human Rights in India: Yesterday Today and Tomorrow, *Tagore Law Lectures*. Eastern Law House, New Delhi.

19. Tyagi, Yogesh K. 1981. "Third World Response to Human Rights," *Indian Journal of International Law*, Vol .21, No.1 (January -March) pp. 120-121.

20. Nizami, Z.A., Devil, Arid. 1994. *Human Rights in the Third World Countries*. Kirs Publications, New Delhi. pp.107.

CHAPTER
4
HUMAN RIGHTS: KEY ISSUES & CHALLENGES

Dr. F. M. Nadaf
Principal
&
Vividh Pawaskar
Head, Department of English
DPM'S Shree Mallikarjun College,
Canacon-GOA

"All human beings, whatever their cultural or historical background, suffer when they are intimidated, imprisoned or tortured... We must, therefore, insist on a global consensus, not only on the need to respect human rights worldwide, but also on the definition of these rights... for it is the inherent nature of all human beings to yearn for freedom, equality and dignity, and they have an equal right to achieve that."

- The Dalai Lama

Introduction

The 2.5 million years of journey of man has been very fascinating. He has passed through many stages such as Homo habilis, Homo erectus, Homo rudolfensis, Homo heidelbergensis, Homo floresiensis and Homo sapiens.

Man spent major part of his life as a nomad moving from one jungle to another jungle.His life was full of hardship as he had no shelter to live and clothes to wear. He lived on trees and caves to protect from harsh weather and animals. Proper food was a major issue as he had no knowledge to grow crops hence; he collected fruits, nuts, roots, flowers, berries from woods and killed animals for food and skin. During this period, human population was very less and the main focus of man was on his security. Hence, no one thought of Human Rights or Civil Rights at that time. The idea of Human Rights gradual began when man entered into the second phase of his journey (nomadic to settled life) and civilizations started flourishing.

The idea of Human Rights did not begin with the establishment of United Nations. But Human Rights are deep-rooted in ancient philosophical thoughts under the concepts of 'Natural Laws' and 'Natural Rights. Hammurabi: the Babylonian King proclaimed a set of commandments to his citizens called 'Hammurabi's Codes.' These codes recognized reasonable wages to its people along with protection to property. Likewise, there is a declaration to rights of humans in the Assyrian Laws, the Hittiti laws, and the Vedic Laws.All religions of the world, despite differences in their philosophy, preach and teach humanist perspective in the light of human rights.

Human rights are those rights, which people normally enjoy because they are humans. In other words, human rights are those rights of the people, which they get automatically on being born as humans.

United Nations opines, "Human rights are rights inherent to all human beings, regardless of race, sex, nationality, ethnicity, language, religion, or any other status. Human rights include the right to life and liberty, freedom from slavery and torture, freedom of opinion and expression, the right to work and education, and many more.Everyone is entitled to these rights, without discrimination".

According to Equality and Human Rights Commission, "Human rights are the basic rights and freedoms that belong to every person in the world, from birth until death. They apply regardless of where you are from, what you believe or how you choose to live your life. They can never be taken away, although they can sometimes be restricted – for example, if a person breaks the law, or in the interests of national security. These basic rights are based on shared values like dignity, fairness, equality, respect, and independence. These values are defined and protected by law".

The Constitution of the Republic of India declares India to be a Sovereign, Socialist, Secular and Democratic Republic. The term 'democratic' symbolizes that the Government gets its power from the will of the people. Indian Constitution guarantees that all are equal irrespective of the race, religion, language, region, sex, and culture. The Preamble of the Constitution of India ledges justice, social, economic and political, liberty of thought, expression, belief, faith and worship, equality of status and of opportunity and fraternity assuring the dignity of the individual and the unity and integrity of the nation to its citizens.

The spectrum of Human Rights is wide enough to cover every imaginable area. The Universal Declaration of Human Rights, born under the guidance of Eleanor Roosevelt (then-first lady of the United States), lists the following Human Rights: "Right to Equality; Freedom from Discrimination; Right to Life, Liberty, Personal Security; Freedom from Slavery; Freedom from Torture and Degrading Treatment; Right to Recognition as a Person before the Law; Right to Equality before the Law; Right to Remedy by Competent Tribunal; Freedom from Arbitrary Arrest and Exile; Right to Fair Public Hearing; Right to be Considered Innocent until Proven Guilty; Freedom from Interference with Privacy, Family, Home and Correspondence; Right to Free Movement in and out of the Country; Right to Asylum in other Countries from Persecution; Right to a Nationality and the Freedom to Change It; Right to Marriage and Family; Right to Own Property; Freedom of Belief and Religion; Freedom of Opinion and Information; Right of Peaceful Assembly and Association; Right to Participate in Government and in Free Elections; Right to Social Security; Right to Desirable Work and to Join Trade Unions; Right to Rest and Leisure; Right to Adequate Living Standard; Right to Education; Right to Participate in the Cultural Life of Community; Right to a Social Order that Articulates this Document; Community Duties Essential to Free and Full Development; And Freedom from State or Personal Interference in the above Rights." From these listed Human Rights, it transpires that the Human Rights are based on dignity, equality and mutual respect- regardless of your nationality, your religion or your beliefs.

Interestingly, the idea that human beings should have a set of basic rights and freedoms has deep roots in Britain. Landmark developments in Britain include the Magna Carta of 1215; the Habeas Corpus Act of 1679 and the Bill of Rights of 1689. And yet, Britain had set out to conquer the world and India is a testimony to its atrocities. Perhaps, Indians did not fall within the ambit of being humans.

Mahatma Gandhi, who is considered as the 'Father of the Nation' for his role in achieving freedom from the British Rule was averse to the idea of Rights Discourse within the Western Tradition and when the famous writer H. G. Wells drew up a list of Human Rights, Gandhi told him that he could do better by drawing up a list of Duties as opposed to Rights: "Begin with a Charter of Duties of Man...and I promise that Rights will follow as Spring follows Winter." Thus, the Gandhian Ideal construes Duties of Man as of paramount importance as compared to the Human Rights that one wishes to enjoy.

In the few centuries, our world has undergone tremendous change in all the spheres. Population of the Globe has increased multifariously. Population that was just 200,000,00 in 1 A,D, has increased to 7,632,819,325 in 2018. This disturbing increase in population has resulted into worldwide economic crisis, political instability, cultural abnormality, racial discrimination, gender inequality, crippling poverty, literacy, communism, widespread unemployment, cyber-attacks, terrorism, and imperialism. These issues have led to denial and violation of Human Rights. There are several concerns those need to be addressed, due to the global instances of human rights violations. Hence, this paper makes an attempt to examine the major issues and challenges related to Human Rights.

GLOBAL ISSUES & CHALLENGES

Following are some of the key issues and challenges of Human Rights across the World:

Rights of the Differently-abled

Disability is a condition of impairment of physical, sensory, cognitive, intellectual, mental, developmental, or some blend of these. Disability significantly affects individuals' life and maybe by birth or may occur during an individuals' lifetime.

According to WHO, about 15 percent of the global populace lives with some kind of disability, of whom 2 to 4 percent experience major complications in functioning. A huge chunk of the disabled population lives in developing and under-developed countries.

Differently-abled people face numerous problems in day-to-day life some of them includes Inaccessibility, Low Representation in Jobs, Barriers to Health Care, Non-inclusive Education System, Attitudinal Barriers, Inaccessible communication systems, Institutional Barriers, Inadequate Data & Statistics, and Poor Implementation of Schemes. These issues are largely prevalent in developing countries whereas the governments in developed countries are highly sensitive to the needs of differently-abled people.

In 2006, United Nations Convention adopted the Rights of Persons with Disabilities. This upholds that all individuals with disabilities are entitled to enjoy all types of human rights and freedoms. A lot has to be done in this regard. There is a need to make our School, Colleges, Universities, Offices,

Workplaces, Buses, Trains, Banking Services and other facilities disabled friendly.

One of its path-breaking achievements, Government of India enacted a law for the differently-abled persons, which is popularly known as Rights of Persons with Disabilities (RPWD) Act, 2016. In his law, Government has identified 21 categories of disabilities. This Law provides direction for the inclusive growth of disabled population.

Hon. Supreme Court of India strongly directed all the higher educational institutions to comply with the provisions of Section 32 of RPWD Act while admitting students each year.

National Centre for Promotion of Employment for Disabled People (NCPEDP) is playing an important role in India. NCPEDPis a cross-disability, non-profit organization, working as an interface between the Government, Industry, International Agencies, and the Voluntary Sector towards empowerment of persons with disabilities.

Women's Rights

Crime against women is widespread in the world. News in the daily newspapers is incomplete without mention to rapes, gang rapes, molestation, acid attacks, domestic violence, bride burning, honor killings, kidnapping, forced child marriage, and violence on a bigger scale including mob violence, and war rapes.

The Gender equality is enshrined in our Constitution. Hence, to uphold and implement the Constitution, Government has passed several laws and taken steps to safeguard equal rights, check social discrimination & various forms of violence and atrocities. But the atrocities and violence against women and children are on the rise despite strong laws such as death penalty for rape. There are cases, where small children aged less than one year are also raped. It is a shame on the humanity.

According to the National Crime Records Bureau, during 2016, a total of 3,38,954 cases of crime against women were reported in India as compared to 3,29,243in the year 2015, and 3,39,457 in 2014, thus showing a slight decline in the cases from 2014 to 2016.

The United Nations is working for the Women Empowerment through its entity for Gender Equality and the Empowerment of Women, also known as UN Women. The major contributions of United Nations in protecting the rights of women include:

- Special Measures for Gender Equality in the United Nations

- Convention on the Elimination of All Forms of Discrimination Against Women

- Declaration on the Elimination of Discrimination against Women

- Declaration on the Elimination of Violence Against Women

- EGM: prevention of violence against women and girls

- Global Implementation Plan to End Violence against Women and Girls

- HeForShe

- NGO Committee on the Status of Women, New York

- United Nations Development Fund for Women

- United Nations International Research and Training Institute for the Advancement of Women

- United Nations Security Council Resolution 1325

- Istanbul Convention

- Gender Equality Architecture Reform

- Despite serious global efforts of United Nations and other countries of the World, the crime against women is on the rise. This trend is not good for the future of humanity.

Human Trafficking

Human Trafficking which is popularly known as 'modern-day-slavery' is one of the oldest, largest and fastest growing organized crimes in the world. Human Trafficking is unlawful, forced and fraudulent trade of men, women, and children for bonded labour, prostitution, begging, child labour or drug trafficking.

United Nations Human Rights Commission / Trafficking Protocol, defines the term "trafficking in persons" as follows:

(a) "Trafficking in persons" shall mean the recruitment, transportation, transfer, harbouring or receipt of persons, by means of the threat or use of force or other forms of coercion, of abduction, of fraud, of deception, of the abuse of power or of a position of vulnerability or of the giving or receiving of payments or benefits to achieve the consent of a person having control over another person, for the purpose of exploitation. Exploitation shall include, at a minimum, the exploitation of the prostitution of others or other forms of sexual exploitation, forced labour or services, slavery or practices similar to slavery, servitude or the removal of organs; (b) The consent of a victim of trafficking in persons to the intended exploitation set forth in subparagraph (a) of this article shall be irrelevant where any of the means set forth in subparagraph (a) have been used; ... (art. 3). The three key elements that must be present for a situation of trafficking in persons (adults) to exist are, therefore: (i) action (recruitment, ...); (ii) means (threat, ...); and (iii) purpose (exploitation).

A large chunk of population, especially, belonging to the disadvantaged sections of society, fall victim to this because of poor economic conditions.

Human trafficking is not only prevalent within a country but people are smuggled internationally. United Nations Office on Drugs and Crime is making all-out efforts to prevent human trafficking and protecting victims but the crime is on the rise.

The legal efforts of India in this direction include Immoral Trafficking Prevention Act (ITPA), the Child Labour Act, Bonded Labour Abolition Act, and the Juvenile Justice Act.

Racism

On the basis of physical traits, human beings are classified into five major racial groups namely, Caucasoid, Negroid,

Capoid, Mongoloid, and Australoid. When we look into the history of human migration, it is evident that the migration of humans began from Africa about One Lakh Seventy Five years back whereas, *Homo sapiens* had occupied entire Africa about One Lakh Fifty Thousand Years ago. It is apparent from various studies that human population migrated from Africa into Europe, Asia, Australia, America and other parts of the World. It means originally entire population belonged to one race. Later, people acquired different characteristics due to geographical conditions of the place in which they moved resulting in different groups.

In the 21st century, though the world has become a global village and all of us have become global citizens, racism has become a serious matter concern resulting inhuman rights violations. It is a matter of fact that racism is present in all societies. The idea of discrimination arises because one race thinks superior to the other race. Discriminations are visible at many places such as educational institutes, at workplaces, and in government offices. Cultures with low levels of tolerance for other racial groups have experienced violent cases.

United Nations is tirelessly working to bring an end to racial discrimination in the World. Some of its efforts include the International Convention on the Elimination of All Forms of Racial Discrimination and the Durban Declaration.

Infanticide

The most vital issue of human rights violation is the Infanticide of the female child. It is taking place throughout the world in different intensity. Infanticide of the female child encompasses either refusing a child, the right to live after the birth or the right to be born, which, amounts to deliberate murder of the child.

The issue of Infanticide is highly predominant in the Continents of South America, Africa, Asia, and Oceania where large-scale gender biases are prevalent. Whereas, it is not a concern in Europe and North America. India is no exception to this. The state like Haryana, Delhi, Rajasthan, and Punjab are notorious for this. The killing of Girl Child is predominant in this part of India. For the last few years, sex ratio is continuously falling in these states.

Rights of the People with AIDS

According to UNAIDS, about 36.7 million people, including 2.1 million children were living with HIV infection globally in 2016. Every year about 1.8 million people are added to this list at a rate of 5000 new infections per day. It is disturbing to note that India has the third highest number of infected population in the world. These are indeed frightening figures. But what is more important is the serious human rights violations. AIDS is viewed as a taboo, and stigma. Despite large numbers of AIDS awareness movements, there are many misconceptions about HIV/AIDS because of which, HIV infected people face social denunciation, discrimination and, social seclusion. The innocent children infected with this virus are the most affected section of the society. These children cannot take admissions in the Schools.

Child Abuse

Child abuse is another form of human rights violation present in our societies irrespective of countries. Child abuse denies a child of the right to live tranquillity, and without any fear.

Child abuse occurs in many ways such as physical abuse, Mental Abuse, Sexual Abuse, Child Neglect, Substance Abuse, and Child Exploitation.

No place is safe for our children because child abuse takes place in schools, at homes or in playgroups. It is generally observed that a large number of children who undergo child abuse belong to socially underprivileged sections of the society.

As per the Ministry of Women and Child Development (MWCD), about 170 million children in India are susceptible to or suffering from difficult circumstances, such as violence at home, separation from family and street life.

All the Governments of the World and the United Nations through its various agencies is working hard to end child abuse but child abuses are rampant in our societies. The major child protection issues include Gender Discrimination, Caste discrimination, Disability, Female foeticide, Infanticide, Domestic violence, Child sexual abuse, Child marriage, Child labour, Child prostitution, Child trafficking, Child sacrifice, Corporal Punishment in schools, Examination Pressure and Student Suicides, Natural disasters, War and conflict and HIV/AIDS.

Terrorism

Today the major population of the world is living under the shadow of terrorism. Terrorism has shattered lives of the people across the world. Despite such an impact of terrorism, there is no universal definition of terrorism. For the academic purpose, terrorism may be defined as attaining religious, ideological or political objectives by the use of violence or threat of violence. Pakistan, Afghanistan, some African Nations and Arabian countries have become the modern-day fountains of terrorism. These are the places from where terror is exported to other countries of the world. India is the most badly affected countries in the world.

In the terror affected countries, terrorism is responsible for the violation of basic human rights of people to live in peace, harmony, and prosperity. Terrorists commit acts such as killing, looting, raping, kidnapping, and human trafficking. According to the Global Terrorism Data, World from 1970 onwards has experienced about 1,70,000 terrorist attack, more than 83,000 bombings, 18,000 assassinations, and 11,000 kidnappings. Hence, there is an urgent need to protect human rights with effective counter-terrorism efforts.

Climate Change

Earth is about 4600 million-year-old planet. On this planet, society and nature are interconnected to one another. Men and women reside in the kingdom of nature and both interact. Nature has a great influence on human beings and human beings have the capacity to modify their surroundings positively or negatively. Any man-made modification in the environment can result in devastating effects and can also pose a danger to the mankind.

Over the years it is observed that the dynamic equilibrium between man and nature is getting distressed resulting into ecological issues such as Global Warming, Climate Change, Sea Level Rise, Deforestation, Desertification, Extinct of Species' Droughts, Flooding, etc.

According to NASA, "Global warming" refers to the long-term warming of the planet. Global temperature shows a well-documented rise since the early 20th century and most notably since the late 1970s. Worldwide, since 1880 the average surface temperature has risen about 1 °C (about 2 °F), relative to the mid-20th-century baseline (of 1951-1980). This is on top of about an additional 0.15 °C of warming from between 1750 and 1880.

Similarly, according to NASA, "Climate change" encompasses global warming, but refers to the broader range of changes that are happening to our planet. These include rising sea levels, shrinking mountain glaciers, accelerating ice melt in Greenland, Antarctica and the Arctic, and shifts in flower/plant blooming times. These are all consequences of the warming, which is caused mainly by people burning fossil fuels and putting out heat-trapping gases into the air. The terms "global warming" and "climate change" are sometimes used interchangeably, but strictly they refer to slightly different things.

Due to Global Warming and Climate Change, our Earth is experiencing extreme weather conditions and natural disasters. Heat waves, droughts, floods, cyclones, birth of new viruses are becoming common in all the continents including America and Europe.

According to some estimates, about 50 percent of the world's population lives below poverty line. Population that is living under poverty has least contributed to the emission of greenhouse gases. But they will be the worst affected by Climate Change and Global Warming. About 60 percent of the population of the Earth resides along the coast. With the rise in the sea level, huge population will be destabilized.

People will lose their homes, jobs, and all the valuables and become refugees in their own land. The human rights will be at the stake.

Global Warming and Climate Change, directly and indirectly, threaten the human rights including the rights to life, rights to water and sanitation, rights to food, rights to health, rights to housing etc.

The negative impacts of climate change are disproportionately borne by persons and communities already in disadvantageous situations owing to geography, poverty, gender, age, disability, cultural or ethnic background, among others, that have historically contributed the least to greenhouse gas emissions. In particular, persons, communities, and even entire States that occupy and rely upon low-lying coastal lands, tundra and Arctic ice, arid lands, and other delicate ecosystems and at risk territories for their housing and subsistence face the greatest threats from climate change. Hence, climate change needs a comprehensive rights-based response. Internationally, many efforts have been made to minimize the impact of climate change. The preamble of the Paris Agreement to the UN Framework Convention on Climate Change clearly underlines to all the countries that whenever action is taken to address Climate Change, respect, promote and consider their respective obligations on human rights.

Conclusion

Other than above-highlighted concerns, right to food, right to clothing, right to shelter, right to education, right to employment, Land Grabbing, Illegal Immigrants, Asylum Seekers and Refugees, Rights of Prisoners, and Sexual

Orientation Discrimination are the other important human rights issues and challenges. United Nations through its umbrella organization is lending its hands to fight human rights issues taking place all over the world. The responsibility to solve these issues rests with the respective countries to eradicate human right violations but what is required is the political will. Similarly, all the citizens have to shoulder the responsibility in the eradicationand elimination evils leading to the violation of human rights, and in making the world a heaven.

References

1. Arfat, Shabina. 2013. Globalisation and Human Rights: An Overview of its Impact. *"American Journal of Humanities and Social Sciences"*. Vol. 1, No, 1, 2013, 18-24 DOI: 10.11634/ 232907811301270 ISSN 2329-0781 Print/ ISSN 2329-079X Online/ World Scholars http://www.worldscholars.org

2. Bhakhry, Savita. 2006. Children in India and their Rights *"National Human Rights Commission"*. Faridkot House, Copernicus Marg, New Delhi-110 001, India.

3. Elias Olusoji. 2000. The Impact Of Globalisation On Human Rights. Amicus Curiae Issue 28 June 2000.

4. Giusti, Dora & Kulkarni, Aneerudh. 2012. Child Protection in India YOJANANovember, 2012.

5. Ratna, Rani. Human Rights in Indian Culture

6. Mercy, D. 2014. *"International Journal of Humanities Social Sciences and Education"* (IJHSSE) Volume 1, Issue 1, January 2014, pp.33-38 www.arcjournals.org

7. Rehan, Sadia. 2013. Origin and Development of Human Rights in Islam and the West: A Comparative Study. *"International Journal of Social Science and Humanity"*. Vol. 3, No.1, January 2013

8. Sastry, T.S.N. 2011. Introduction to Human Rights And Duties. University of Pune, Ganeshkhind, Pune.

Reports

1. Crime in India 2015 Statistics. National Crime Records Bureau (Ministry of Home Affairs) Government of India East Block - 7, R.K. Puram, New Delhi.

2. Crime in India 2016 Statistics National Crime Records Bureau (Ministry of Home Affairs) Government of India, National Highway–8, Mahipalpur, New Delhi.

3. Human Rights and Human Trafficking Fact Sheet No. 36, 2014. United Nations, New York and Geneva.

Websites

https://www.humanrights.gov.au/news/speeches/human-rights-everyone-everywhere-everyday-2009

https://opinionfront.com/list-of-human-rights-issues

https://www.ohchr.org/EN/Issues/HRAndClimateChange/Pages/HRClimateChangeIndex.aspx

https://ourworldindata.org/extreme-poverty

https://www.globalissues.org/article/4/poverty-around-theworld#WorldBankPovertyEstimatesRevised

https://en.wikipedia.org/wiki/History_oh_human_migration

https://www.hiv.gov/hiv-basics/overview-data-and-trends/global-statistics

https://globalissues.org/article-26/poverty-facts-and-stats

https://www.unwomen.org/en/about-us/about-un-women

https://climate.nasa.gov/faq/

https://www.who.int/topics/disabilities/en/

https://www.unitedforhumanrights.ie/whats-are-human-rights/universal-declaration-of-human-rights/

https://humanorigins.si.edu/education/introduction-human-evolution

CHAPTER 5

HUMAN RIGHTS IN INDIA: THEORY AND PRACTICE

Saroj Kumari

Associate Professor

Department of Political Science

S.N.D.B. Gov P.G. College

Nohar

Hanumangarh

(Rajasthan)

Introduction

Today's is a world of Democracy. Liberty, equality and fraternity are its basic values Man has struggled for ages to attain these and sacrificed a lot. The concept of Human Rights in its present form has originated after 2nd world war. Emphasizing their need, Eleanor Roosevelt, the chairperson of the UN Committee on Human Rights has rightly remarked, "basically we could not have peace or an atmosphere in which peace could grow, unless we recognized the rights of individual human-beings, their importance, their dignity and agreed that was the basic thing that had to be accepted throughout the world". Thus the HR are pertinent and a pre-condition for achieving world peace. If a person is not treated with equality and dignity, his grievances are not redressed properly and in time, then he is bound to be indifferent to the society and becomes violent. Therefore, individual dignity is important and it should be maintained at all.

Human Rights are the most important issue of the day and are the part and parcel of the global peace movement. Theoretically, there is no dispute regarding the need and importance of Human Right to all individuals. Hence, these have been incorporated in democratic constitutions after the Universal Declaration of Human Rights in 1948 and 10th December is celebrated as International Human Rights day. However, the UDHR is only a code of standard not of law. It infers that.. "all people are born free and equal in dignity and right and that they should not be discriminated against because of their nationality, ethnicity, religion, race, gender. Wealth, property and political opinion!' But the situation is not bright and homogeneous so far the practice is concerned, There are innumerable cases of violation of HR both at individual as well as mass levels all over the world!. However, their gravity and number is far more in third world countries as compared to the developed ones. Moreover, persons with poor socio-economic background and from fair gender are the worst affected sections of any society. In the era of globalised economy, affluence of few people has increased multifold due to over-centralization of resources on the one hand and poverty, un-employment, socio-economic dispirited and insecurity have increased on the other. If we look at Indian economy, dramatic changes have been observed in its GDP.

The number of billionaires and millionaires is increasing rapidly both in India and abroad India has become the second most preferential country in the world for foreign direct investment. But these benefits of development have confined to a microscopic number of the population and still more than one-fourth of the population is living below the poverty line and they are becoming poorer day by day The MNC's have thwarted the very existence of the state. Moreover, the state apparatus is still a major violator of HR in 3rd world countries including India where majority of the population is illiterate, ignorant and poor. HR is still a far cry for these people. In India 18 states are suffering from naxalize, terrorism, insurgency besides frequent caste and communal rights. Fatwas or Khap Panchayats, Bonded labour, child labour. Gender discrimination and trafficking of young women. Domestic: and public violence against them, ignorance and apathy towards elderly people are the other form of Human Right violation.

The delayed and expensive judicial process has added in their score. HR are meaningful only when these are applicable and accessible to all citizens. It would be pertinent to quote here Martin Annals, former General Secretary of Amnesty International. Each violation of human rights, wherever it occurs is a threat to the welfare and dignity of the entire human family. The protection of HR therefore. is worldwide responsibility, which transcends all racial. Ideological and geographical boundaries.

Evolution of the Concept

The concept of Human Rights has arisen from that of natural rights of all human. The belief that every person by virtue of his humanity is entitled to certain natural rights is a recurring theme throughout the history of mankind. It can be traced back thousands of years from the Vedas to the Hammurabi Code to the Magna Carta, the French Declaration of Human Rights, and the American Bill of Rights. Time and again history shows that the existence of human rights has been recognised and accepted as a necessary component for the well being of civilisation at any given time. In Ca. 2050 BC, Ur Nammu, the king of Ur created the first legal codex: followed by several other sets of laws in Mesopotamia including the Code of Hammurabai (ca. 1780 BC); one of the best preserved example of the kind. Various rules and punishment on variety of matters including women's rights, children's rights and slave rights are mentioned in the code. The Persian Empire (Iran) established unprecedented principles of human rights in the 6th century BC under the reign of Cyrus. Three centuries later, the Mauryan Empire established principles of civil rights. Religious documents the Vedas, the Bible, the Quran and Analects of Confucius also referred to the duties, rights and responsibilities of the citizens. In 1222, the Manden Charter of Mali was a declaration of essential human rights including the rights to life, and opposed the practice of slavery. Several 17th and 18th century European philosophers developed the concept of natural rights, the notion that people possess certain rights by virtue of being human.

The United States Declaration of Independence includes concept of natural rights and states "that all men are created equal, that they are endowed by their creator with certain unalienable rights, that among these are life, liberty and the pursuit of happiness" The concept of human rights has undergone a revolutionary change since the Magna Charta of

1215 to the rights contained in the Unites Nation Convention.

The charter of United Nations which came into force in October1945 begins with the determination of the people of member nations to save the succeeding generations from the scourge of war and to reaffirm their faith in the fundamental human rights and the dignity of human being. The 'World conference of Human Rights' held in 1993 marks a crucial stage in United Nation's policy in the field of human rights. The Vienna Declaration encouraged the United Nations to pursue and strengthen its activities to make respect for human rights a priority objective on the same level as development and democracy and to work for the concurrent achievements of these three objectives. It is interesting to note that the United Nations 'Commission on Human Rights' also created in 1947, a sub-commission on 'Freedom of Information and of the Press' to report to the 'Commission on Human Rights' on what rights, obligations and practices should constitute the freedom of information. This necessarily had to be juxtaposed with the human rights. Its report on the subject, including the draft code of ethics, was a copious contribution to the charter drawn up subsequently.

Conceptual Framework

What are Human Rights? Is difficult to define the concept in a few words. Harold D. Laski has rightly remarked. The rights are. in fact, those conditions of social life without which no men can seek. in general, to be himself at his best". He further stated. "the quality of a government is determined by the rights, it provides to its citizens". Hence there is no dispute or ambiguity regarding the relevance of HR for mankind. Even after this fact the scholars on the subjects lack anonymity regarding the human rights there are various definitions available on the topic. The ever-rising scope of HR and diversity of opinion regarding its meaning and contents have made it more complex and comprehensive. So far the UDHR (1948) is concerned; it consists of a series of rights. It states that all men are born free having rights, dignity and decency. Hence they have privilege to get every right and liberty. Articles 1 & 2 prohibit any discrimination among people on grounds of religion, caste, creed, language. sex, birth etc. whereas Articles 3 to 21 are concerned with the declaration of civil and political rights.

It includes right to life, liberty and security, freedom from arbitrary arrest, a fair trial. Equal protection of law, freedom and movement, thought. Expression and faith, right to equality and property. Right to nationality and right to seek asylum etc. Similarly articles 22-27 describe the socio-economic and cultural rights including right to social security, right to work and leisure, right to education and participation in cultural activities besides right to health and welfare. Articles 28-30 enumerate that social and international fabric required for attaining these rights and liberties: It also emphasis the rights and duties of each individual in society. Thus the Universal Declaration of Homan Rights is the first segment of the International Bill of Human Rights, which has been supplemented and updated from time to time by various conventions and conferences held on the subject. Therefore, Human Right may be said to be those rights, which are essential for the dignified and decent human existence as well as for the adequate development of human personality. Generally HR is those "fundamental rights to which every man, women inhabiting any part of the world should be deemed entitled by virtue of having born as a human being.

Human Right therefore, is of three categories-(I) civil and political rights for individual against State. (ii) Economic & social rights as a prerequisite for the enjoyment of civil & political rights, (iii) Right to development and have a congenial environment. All the three types of Human Right are inter-linked and complementary to one another.

Statutory Provisions and Practices in India

There are a number of provisions regarding the protection and promotion of Human Rights in Indian constitution prominent among these are the preamble, fundamental rights and Directive Principals of State Policy given in parts III and IV.

Articles 32 and 226 of the constitution provide special safeguards to fundamental rights which comprises of most of Human Rights. Similarly part XVI is concerned with SC and STs and makes elaborate provision for their protection, Safety and development. In addition to this, the parliament and state assemblies have enacted a number of legislations on the topic. The Government of India has established various commissions in 90 for protection of Human Rights. Prominent among these are National Human Right Commission. National Women Commission. National Minority Commission and National Commission of SC and STs. The concept of judicial activism, Public Interest Litigation and human rights organizations are also playing an important role in protection and promotion of Human Right in India.

Human Rights in India have been violated at different intervals by various Factors in different forms. The prominent among this arc poverty, unemployment. Socio-economic disparities illiteracy. Ignorance, inhumane conditions of work in factories and business installations, overburden of work and poor payment, depression. Prostitution, rape, trafficking of young women and children, bonded labour, child labour, discrimination and insecurity to elders, widows, handicapped and other weaker sections of society. Sexual and mental harassment to women, violence in any form. Ever-rising problems of pollution. Violation of human rights by State machinery etc. Laski has rightly remarked that "where economic disparities are glaring high, the relations among citizens will turned into masters and slaves. 'Resources are unevenly divided in Indian society, less than 20% of our population owns and controls more than 80% of the resources and vice-versa.

So far the health and hygienic conditions are concerned. 135 million people have no access to basic health facilities. 126 million are not accessible for safe drinking water and about 70% of the population lack basic sanitation facilities,' Even after having ample natural resources, India has the largest number of diseased, disabled and blind people in the world, The latest statistics issued by a team of doctors working in Delhi under the aegis of WHO give an alarming picture of the situation. It states that- every 5 seconds one person goes blind in the world and a child goes every minute. There are 17.6 million estimated blinds in India. which is largest in the world. Moreover, there are about 150 million blind children in India. most of that blindness can be removed if they simply wore spectacles." The process of LPG has made the things rather worse. About 26% of our population is still living BPL and they are not in a position to meet out their basic needs squarely. What to speak of HR for such people whose very survival and existence is also at stake? Kettering these objectives into considerations, the Govt. of India have launched various programs for removal of poverty and unemployment starting from Community Development Programme (1952) to National Rural Employment Guarantee Act (2006). Billions of rupees have been spent on these programmes to accomplice the poise goal of egalitarian society. But the number and sravity of the poors is increasing instantly.

We have failed to provide adequate jobs to millions of unemployed hands. Until the basic needs of every individual are fulfilled, we cannot boast of a rising and shining India. The LPG process effected Indian economy in every field but all benefits have accrued to just 1 % of our total population and still 26% of the population is living below the poverty line and they are becoming poorer day by day.

Human Rights are still a myth for these people. In India 18 states are suffering from terrorism. In India prominent cast and communal riots are Mandal riots (1990), collapse of Disputed Structure in Ayodhya (1992), Terrorist attack in Bombay (1993), Attack on Red Fort Dec, 22, 2000, J&K assembly attack in October, (2001), Attack on Indian parliament (2001), Godhara Carnage and Best Bakery episode (2002), Terrorist attack in Akshar Dham, Temple Gujrat 24 Sep, 2002, Gohana cases (2005), Gurgoan and Rohtak brutalities (2005), Delhi bomb blasts (2005), Jaipur Bombing May, 13, 2008, Pathankot attack 2 January, 2016, Uri attack Sep, 2016 etc. The delayed, lethargic and highly expensive judicial process has added in the score of HR violation Lakhs of cases are pending in the courts and waiting for their turn for many years. It has become too difficult for an average man to get justice in the present system. HR are meaningful only when these are applicable and accessible to all citizens in practice.

Though the percentage of working women in Indian is still low as compared to the developed nations. The working women have to face a lot of miseries and harassment at their workplace or while they are in commutation. 'We read frequently in newspapers about such incidents of violation of human rights. What to speak of women working in far-flanged areas. even the streets and roads of national capital are not safe. India has the largest number of cases in world regarding genital mutilation of girls. The government has provided a number of safeguards and protection to working women and made strict legislation regarding it. The domestic violation of HR of women is another important aspect which has remained hidden for long. Lust of materialism has increased multifold the cases of discrimination on gender basis. Dowry, divorce, bride burning or murder. Besides strict anti-dowry laws, the Govt. has passed the Domestic Violence Act (2005) and amended the Hindu Succession Act (2005) which gives equal share to daughters in their parental property. However in absence of uniform civil code, Muslim women could not get dignified status in the society. Polygamy and purdah customs are prominent in this community.

The National Commission for Women established in 1993 is performing very well in this direction and has taken serious note of certain cases brought to its notice. SC and STs who constitute about 25.2% of our total population are the other vulnerable segments of Indian society facing violation of HR at larger level. As they are the most exploited, suppressed and deprived sections of the society since ages. Minorities are another section of Indian population who has to face frequent challenges to HR. As India is a heterogeneous society, hence the term 'minority' is very complex and full of ambiguity. Though the constitution provides equal rights to all citizens, yet certain immunities and safeguards have been granted to minorities in the constitution particularly in Part III in articles 25-30. Besides establishment of National Minority Commission in 1992. The Govt. has passed much legislation on the topic However. Some of these have given negative impacts on the society i.e. the Parliament nullified the historic decision of Supreme Court in Sahbano Case where uniform application of Art 44 (unified civil Code) has been emphasized by the court. Similarly the vote bank politics turned into appeasement of minorities without caring of its future consequences. Hindu constitutes about 79.8% of India's population. Still more than 3 lakh Hindu families have to ply from Sri Nagar and are living as refugees in camps. Thus a judicious and broader approach needs to follow it this case. Pollution is another important factor which has threatened our Human Rights.

Conclusion

The apex court of the country in a watershed judgment in the case of Olga Tellis v/s Bombay municipal Corporation declared that a man has not only a right to live but to live with human dignity. Consequently all attributes for living with the dignity of a human soul namely education, shelter etc. are to be guaranteed and welfare activities of the State must be directed to ensure socio-economic condition where no one in the country is deprived of the basic requirements to lead a dignified life. It is the duty of state and society to provide a minimum standard of life to every citizen. Let's hope for a better tomorrow.

References

1. Ennals, Martin. 1986. 'The struggle for Human Rights', A. R. Desai (ed.), Violation of Human rights in India, (Bombay Popular, vol1) p 3.

2. India Today, 11/1/2006. Pp 20-26.

3. India Today, 26/11/2014.

4. Bashu D.D, Indian Constution.

5. Kashyap, Subhash Indian Govt. and Politics.

6. Jain, Rajesh. 2005. New Trends of Indian Politics. College Book Depot, Jaipur.

7. Kashyap, S.C. 1978.Human Rights & Parliament. Metropolitan, Delhi.pp. 2.

8. Moorthy, P. 2005. "Promotion of Human Rights Today: Problems and Prospects", Journal of Political Science, vol. 1(2), (Jalandhar : DAV College. pp. 51-52.

9. National Herold, New Delhi, 13 October, 2000.

10. Olga Tellis v/s Bombay municipal Corporation (1985) 3 SCC 545.

11. Rajasthan Patrika, 20/05/2007.

12. Schramm, Wilbur. 2002. Mass Communication, Illinois

Uni. Press, 1960: Kewal J. Kumar, Mass Communication in India. Jaico Pub., Mumbai. pp. 41.

13. The Pioneer, New Delhi, 13 October, 2000.

14. The Tribune, 17/01/2010.

15. The Tribune, 24/01/2012.

16. The Tribune, 26/12/2013.

CHAPTER
6

ERA OF GLOBALIZATION AND STATUS OF HUMAN RIGHTS

Dr. Shyam S. Khinchi
Associate Professor & Head
Department of Geography
Dr. Bhim Rao Ambedkar Govt. P.G. College,
Sri Ganganagar
(Rajasthan)

Dr. Jai Singh Rathore
Associate Professor
Department of Geography
Jai Narain Vyas University,
Jodhpur
(Rajasthan)

Introduction

Global human rights law points basically to shield people and gatherings from oppressive activity by states and state specialists. Late improvements all through the world, including fizzled states, monetary deregulation, privatization, and exchange advancement crosswise over fringes parts of what has come to be known as globalization have prompted to the development of effective non-state performing artists who have assets once in a while more noteworthy than those of many states. Two restricting perspectives of globalization and its relationship to human rights have risen: some observe the two subjects as commonly fortifying and positive in enhancing human prosperity, while others see globalization as posturing new dangers not satisfactorily administered by existing universal human rights law.

Globalization

In the year 1999 Human Rights Development Report, the United Nations Development Program characterizes globalization as contracting space, contracting time, and vanishing of fringes. Characterized thusly, globalization gives off an impression of being a procedure that is age old, nonstop, and irreversible. "Globalization" is currently generally used to entirety up today's reality arrange. It implies they progressively coordinate the world into one industrialist political economy working under a neo-liberal free market philosophy. In this unique situation, globalization implies worldwide monetary advancement, building up a worldwide money related framework and a transnational generation framework which depends on a homogenized overall law of significant worth. A generally acknowledged meaning of globalization incorporates financial, as well as political, social, social, and innovative co-operations crosswise over nations. At the end of the day, globalization likewise speaks to the spread of thoughts, data, values and individuals, going past the stream of products, capital and administrations or market trades.

Globalization Connect and Human Rights

The legal relationship between globalization and human rights can be analyzed from the perspective of economic regulation as well as that of human rights law, examining first whether international economic law sufficiently supports or takes into account human rights concerns, then considering the extent to which human rights law takes into account globalization and economic interests. In respect to both inquiries, the fundamental question is whether a human rights system premised on state responsibility to respect and ensure human rights can be effective in a globalized world.

Effect of Globalization on Society

Globalization is a huge calculate aggressive world that coordinate and prepare social estimations of individuals at worldwide level. In the period of fast specialized movement, numerous nations are bound together and changed because of the procedure of globalization. Globalization huge affects social, social, money related, political, and collective existence of nations. Copious hypothetical reviews showed that globalization mediates in a social existence of masses that raises various basic issues (Robertson, 1992). In expansive sense, the expression "globalization" implies mix of economies and social orders through cross country streams of data, thoughts, advancements, products, administrations, capital, fund and individuals. Globalization is depicted by scholars as the procedure through which social orders and economies are incorporated through cross outskirt streams of thoughts, correspondence, innovation, capital, individuals, fund, merchandise, administrations and data.

Effect of Globalization and It's Effect

Numerous scholars stated that adjustment in environment has both positive and negative perspectives (Harris, 2002). These invigorate driving or opposing strengths toward the change of the present state of affairs. This is most clear with respect to both globalization, and the subsequent spread of the worldwide association. There are four elements that quicken globalization.

The market basic: Impact on national economies of bigger, transnational markets portrayed by free, convertible monetary standards, open access to saving money, and contracts enforceable by law.

The asset basic: Growing association of countries and their exercises on each other, encouraged by the consumption of characteristic assets, misdistributions of arable land, mineral assets, and riches, and overpopulation. The undeveloped countries require the capital, innovation, and mental aptitude of the wealthier nations, while the First World economies are logically reliant on the characteristic and HR of the creating countries.

The IT basic: Modernizations in glob correspondences, science and innovation contribute toward universalization or planarization.

The biological goal: Globalization has extraordinary impact on the ecologies and situations of countries which need to protections that decrease the negative impacts as opposed to abusing without respect to such concerns.

India was fundamental mover of globalization. The administration of India made significant alterations in its financial approach in 1991 by which it permitted coordinate outside interests in the nation. Thus, globalization of the Indian Industry happened everywhere scale. In India, financial extension was seen in nineteenth century because of significant emergency drove by remote trade. The advancement of the household economy and upgraded joining of India with the gross domestic product (GDP) development rates which made great position in worldwide scale. Impacts of globalization in Indian Industry are seen as this procedure got a lot of outside ventures into the business particularly in the BPO, pharmaceutical, petroleum, and assembling enterprises. Therefore, they supported the Indian economy fundamentally. The advantages of the impacts of globalization in the Indian Industry are that numerous outside organizations set up ventures in India, particularly in the pharmaceutical, BPO, petroleum, assembling, and synthetic areas and this offered extraordinary open doors for work to Indian individuals. Likewise this decreased the level of unemployment and neediness in the nation. It is watched that the significant strengths of globalization in India has been in the improvement of outsourced IT and business handle outsourcing administrations. Since last numerous years, there is an expansion of talented experts in India utilized by both nearby and remote organizations to administration clients in the US and Europe. These nations exploit India's lower taken a toll yet exceptionally capable and English-talking work compel, and uses worldwide correspondences advancements, for example, voice-over IP (VOIP), email and the web, global endeavors have possessed the capacity to bring down their cost base by setting up outsourced learning specialist operations in India. The remote organizations got profoundly propelled innovation with them and this made the Indian Industry all the more innovatively progressed. Globalization in India has been helpful for organizations that have wandered in the Indian market. It is prescribed by analysts that India needs to concentrate on five vital regions to improve its financial status. The ranges incorporate mechanical business, new business openings for little and medium endeavors, the significance of value administration, new prospects in country regions and privatization of money related foundations.

Following are the some other examples

1. The alterations proposed by the administration in laws identified with remote speculation, exchange unions, contract work, processing plants, modern debate, and monopolistic practices, impact affect human rights, particularly the human privileges of workers and ladies laborers.

2. A Non-Governmental Organization that the soda pops produced by Pepsi and Coca-Cola contained poisonous pesticides, the legislature quickly prohibited their deal inside Parliament however left the strength of customary shoppers helpless before corporate deception. A Joint Parliamentary Committee researched the matter and recommended encircling fitting rules, which have not been actualized to date. Subsequently, very little has changed even as late test reports affirmed the nearness of abnormal state of pesticides in sodas. All things

considered, the focal government has not yet made any therapeutic move and corporate bodies have turned out to shield included enterprises in fighting that any sweeping restriction on the offer of soda pops will antagonistically influence the speculation atmosphere.

3.   The administration has indicated undue tolerance, and in this manner sent a wrong flag, to outside partnerships in regards to their human rights obligation by not vivaciously seeking after the removal of Warren Anderson, the ex-CEO of Union Carbide Corporation, against whom criminal procedures are pending under the watchful eye of a court in connection to the Bhopal gas disaster.

With the procedure of globalization, there is an entrance to TV developed from 20% of the urban populace to 90% of the urban populace. Indeed, even in the provincial regions satellite TV has a grown up market. In the urban areas, Internet office is all over and augmentation of web offices even to rustic territories. There is an expansion of worldwide natural way of life/eateries in the urban territories of India. Over the top Multiplex film corridors, enormous shopping centers and skyscraper private are found in each urban area. Diversion division in India has a worldwide market. After monetary progression, Bollywood extended its region and demonstrated a noteworthy nearness in the worldwide scale. The business started to investigate better approaches to end up distinctly more worldwide and cutting edge. In India, innovation is seen with the West. Subsequently, Western logic started to be consolidated into Bollywood movies. As these new social messages started to achieve the Indian populace, Indian moviegoers were pushed to re-assess their conventional Indian social belief system. Bollywood films are additionally circulated and acknowledged at worldwide level. Huge global organizations are contributing on this division. Acclaimed International brands, for example, Armani, Gucci, Nike, and Omega are likewise making interest in the Indian market with the changing of mold explanation of Indians.

There are some negative effect of globalization, for example, this procedure made uniqueness amongst rustic and urban Indian joblessness, development of ghetto capitals and risk of fear monger exercises. Globalization expanded rivalry in the Indian market between the outside organizations and residential organizations. With the remote products being superior to the Indian merchandise, the buyer wanted to purchase the outside products. This lessened the measure of benefit of the Indian Industry organizations. This happened chiefly in the pharmaceutical, assembling, compound, and steel businesses. The negative Effects of Globalization on Indian Industry are that with the happening to innovation the quantity of work required are diminished and this came about expanding unemployment particularly in the field of the pharmaceutical, concoction, assembling, and concrete ventures. Some segments of individuals in India that are poor don't get advantage of globalization. There is an expanded hole amongst rich and poor that prompts to some criminal exercises. Moral duty of business has been lessened. Another significant negative impact of globalization in India is that adolescents of India leaving their reviews early and joining Call focuses to gain quick cash lessening their social life in the wake of getting habituated with dull work. There is an expansion of each day by day usable ware. This adverse effects social angle. The foundation of marriage is separating at quick rate. There are more individuals moving toward separation courts as opposed to keeping up conjugal life. Globalization has significant effect on the religious circumstance of India. Globalization has achieved raising a populace who is rationalist and skeptic. Individuals going by spots of love are decreasing with time. Globalization has lessened patriotism and patriotism in nation.

Human Rights Good for Globalization

The dominant view among economists and policy makers in multilateral financial institutions appears to be that any hindrances to global trade and investment are bad for development in general. Recent studies, however, suggest that business and economic indicators are better in developing countries that have more favorable civil and political rights than in repressive regimes. Mancur Olson explains that the majority in whose interests a democratic government is ruling demand smaller growth-retarding exaction from the minority and pay greater attention to the supply of growth-promoting public goods than does a dictatorship, even when the majority is acting out of pure self-interest. According to his analysis, the dispersal of political power and the emergence of representative government have often been the trigger for faster economic growth. So, prosperity is not only good for democracy, but democracy seems good for prosperity. A feature in the poorest countries is the absence or poor enforcement of contract and property rights, which are necessary for advanced markets and rapid growth.It also seems clear that establishment of the rule of law with protection for contracts and property rights are essential to maintaining security for international investment and trade. Tourism is the world's fastest-growing industry, generating more than 10% of total international GNP, and is particularly harmed by images of repression, acts of terrorism, and the political instability that usually result from widespread human rights abuses. Judicial reform and the establishment of the rule of law with respect for human rights should be a priority, even if only for the instrumental reason to secure investment, property, contracts, debts, and profits. As the U.N. Development Program's Human Development Report 2000 proclaims, "rights make human beings better economic actors."

Like human rights, economic liberalization is concerned with restraining the power of the state. At the special session of the U.N. General Assembly to review progress since the 1995 Copenhagen World Summit for Social Development, the final document, adopted on July 1, 2000, makes special reference to the role and responsibilities of the private sector to work with governments to eradicate poverty, promote full employment and universal access to social services, and ensure that everyone has equal opportunities to participate in society. In turn, democratic rule and the rule of law inspire further global business activity, generating an upward spiral in rights protection. The text encourages corporate social responsibility and promotes dialogue among government, labor, and employer groups. It also expresses a belief in the relationship between economic growth and social development. The Copenhagen Declaration and Program of Action affirmed that social development and social justice cannot be attained in the absence of respect for all human rights and fundamental freedoms. The Sub-Commission on Promotion and Protection of Human Rights finds in major human rights instruments "obligations and goals which are fundamental to the development process and to economic policy". None of the international human rights instruments imposes an economic model, free trade, or deregulation. Yet, as Anne or ford points out, there is a link between human rights and a liberal economic regime that may facilitate globalization. Liberal concepts of human rights identify the individual with property ownership and are linked with the emergence of capitalism. In contrast, the failure by some governments to respect core labor standards is likely to provoke trade tensions and lead to protectionist efforts. The stability of the world's trading system may thus depend upon ensuring that an open trading system does not come at the price of human rights.

Positive Effect of Globalization on Human Rights

On the constructive side, the expanding financial holes have alarmed individuals to since quite a while ago dismissed social and monetary rights. When all is said in done, exchange hypothesis predicts a noteworthy increment in worldwide welfare coming from globalization, in a roundabout way upgrading the accomplishment of financial conditions fundamental for monetary and social rights. It is trusted that market systems and changed exchange will prompt to a change in the expectations for everyday comforts surprisingly. Organized commerce and financial opportunity are fundamental states of political flexibility, or if nothing else add to the decide of law that is a basic part of human rights.

Positively, globalization encourages universal trades that beat the limits of a solitary country or a human advancement, permitting investment in a worldwide group. There is additionally the likelihood that financial power can be used to authorize human rights violators all the more viably.

Another imperative advancement is the expanding regard for ladies' rights and joining of "ladies' human rights" into the human rights talk. Exchange and FDI decidedly influence ladies' work openings in creating nations, because of their relative favorable circumstances. As it were, creating nations have a near favorable position in labor-concentrated merchandise, therefore interest for female work would increment keeping in mind the end goal to keep value intensity in universal exchange as female wages are by and large lower.

Globalization has likewise made some monetary open doors for ladies. All things considered, expanding investment of ladies in the economy, regardless of the possibility that it is generally in the casual part holds the capability of engaging a few ladies.

Negative Effect of Globalization on Human Rights

Globalization has considerably added to the increase of obligation, neediness and financial emergency in the creating scene. The Structural Adjustment Programs planned and forced by the worldwide loan boss foundations is a normal instrument to make an ideal environment for globalization, which at last influences creating nations. More cash is being spent on fare introduction, which brings about nearby economies getting to be distinctly subject to the coordination with the world economy. The universal banks request poor economies to redirect considerable assets far from divisions serving household needs: pull back all endowments for destitute individuals, privatize the state area, deregulate the market, and reduction compensation. In actuality, this procedure opens up nations to globalization. In this way basic change projects and import-trade drove methodologies of industrialization were a piece of a political and monetary rebuilding process, a prelude to globalization.

The supporters of globalization give philosophical avocations to acknowledge send out drove development, bring down wages and expectations for everyday comforts for specialists, contracting government spending plans, and amazingly high financing costs. Intense establishments like the International Monetary Fund, the World Bank and the World Trade Organization raise the TINA, contention to convince the creating countries to qualify themselves to get cash. The forming nations are left into no alternative however to acknowledge the progression and market-arranged changes. Under this advancement approach creation has a tendency to be fare arranged. Meeting the essential needs of the general population turn out to be less imperative. State-run manufacturing plants or undertakings are regularly privatized to suit the requirements of remote financial specialists. Unhindered commerce and progression prompt to rivalry and nearby makers, similar to ranchers, need to endure the outcomes. In this manner, financial improvement with value remains a delusion for the poor populace in spite of a huge number of advancement measures received by the legislature.

A social lobbyist of the Philippines, remarks that similarly that colonization was the pattern one hundred years back, globalization is, today. Today worldwide companies have supplanted the pilgrim powers. In creating nations, worldwide companies are permitted to devour normal assets, HR, and national riches. They dislodge ranchers from their territory, laborers from their employments, and groups from their foundations. They are in charge of the separating of groups and the pulverization of the earth to serve the human and crude material prerequisites of worldwide creation for the worldwide market. The outcome is the crumple of nourishment security and the development of worldwide ecological emergencies, which at last may end up being far more detestable than colonization. Indeed, even the people groups of created nations experience the ill effects of the benefit hungry standards of worldwide companies today, which for all intents and purposes lead the world.

The prompt indication of the appearing incongruence of the estimation of financial productivity vis-a-vis human rights is what is known as advancement hostility, i.e. where "monetary choices take practically zero record of human and ecological costs, that are arranged and executed from the top and without investment of those concerned, and that are forced on individuals either by drive or by denying them of the fundamental data and intends to settle on a genuine decision".

Doubtlessly the boundless infringement of human rights is identified with the extending crevice between the rich and poor people, both on the worldwide and on the neighborhood levels. Worldwide Statistics demonstrate that a large portion of the world almost three billion individuals live on under two dollars a day; the wealthiest country on earth has the vastest hole amongst rich and poor of any industrialized country; the top fifth of the world's kin in the wealthiest nations appreciate 82% of the growing fare exchange and 68% of remote direct speculation while the base fifth, scarcely over 1%. This prompts to an expanding sentiment hardship and bad form among the populaces of the diverse nations of the world. The denied are uncovered day by day, if not each moment to pictures and proofs of the tremendous crevice in ways of life between the rich and poor people.

The non-state performing artists in particular the media, companies, global associations like the World Bank and the WTO have developed as pseudo-focuses of administrative and control systems in social and monetary exercises. This pseudo-anti-extremism has been thusly made by globalization consequently releasing the real control instruments of the legislature.

Conclusion

Each nation is a performing artist during the time spent globalization and a creating economy like India is no special case to it. Obviously, it has turned out to be basic for all the nations to acknowledge the imperfections made by globalization. All around, human rights have been undermined in the globalized period as is apparent from its different negative impacts.

As said over, the disadvantages of globalization have dwarfed the benefits in a few cases. The developing disparities regarding essential needs of a human have been brought about subsequently of globalization. As has been talked about before, globalization has neglected to create a comprehensive financial improvement. Advancement of business sectors is expected to right awkward nature in destitution mitigation measures, arrangement of free and obligatory essential instruction, enhanced nourishment and territorial balance in arrangement of administrations which are the fundamental privileges of a person. Unexpectedly, progression has, actually, very profited the restricted top levels of the business sectors deserting the wide base levels of business sectors which are not really ready to confront the solid rivalries to which they have been uncovered, with outside players. This has constrained the indigenous individuals occupied with business exercises to make new developments from time to time to charm the customers who have been gotten under the grip of exploitative consumerism. Without a doubt, globalization has taken after just the top-down approach as against the base down approach which is the need of great importance. The LPG idea has made it essential for India to truly adjust to the deficiencies in the present society and later on too. In this way, there is a prompt earnestness for every one of the legislatures to casing laws and strategies organizing privileges of individuals over globalization in the coming years as there is each likelihood of the human rights to be debilitated in some frame or the other in the post-globalized period.

References

1. Bertr and Ramcharan, G. 2008. *"Contemporary Human Rights Ideas."* London and New York: Routledge, pp. 34-36,

2. Glenda T. Litong. 2004. "Making A Case For Human Rights In The Context Of Globalization Or Vice Versa?" http://aprnet.org/,Jun.04,2004. Available:http://www.aprnet.org/index.php/conferences-aworkshop/45-regional-economic cooperation-andhuman-rights-in-

asia/176making-a-case-for-humanrights-in-the-context-of-globalization-or-vice-versa.

3. Jha, Anil Kumar. 2012. *"Gender Inequality and Women Empowerment."* Axis Books Pvt. Ltd., New Delhi, pp.51-58.

4. Patil, V.T. 2001. *"Human Rights-Third Millennium Vision."* Authors Press Publications, New Delhi, pp.273-285.

5. Prabhash, J. 2011. "Human Rights in a Globalized World: Market Friendly Rights vs. People Friendly Rights, A Theoretical Construct." in *Human Rights in a Changing World*, P. Sukumaran Nair (eds.). Kalpaz Publications, New Delhi, pp. 45-49.

6. Sapru, R. K. 2006. *"Public Policy: Formulation, Implementation and Evaluation."* Sterling Publishers Pvt. Ltd., New Delhi. pp. 280-288.

CHAPTER
7

PROBLEM AND PROSPECTS OF CHILDREN RIGHTS IN INDIA

Meenu Tanwar
Associate Professor & Head
Department of Sociology,
Ch. Ballu Ram Godara Govt. Girls P.G. College,
Sri Ganganagar
(Rajasthan)

Introduction

India is the second largest population country in the world after China and huge number of children in India. The number of inhabitants in children's in India is around thirty-five million of the aggregate populace. Destitution frequently referred to as the most well-known ground for the infringement of the privileges of children's in India. Besides, absence of value instruction and separation particularly towards the socially in reverse individuals of the nation constitutes as a noteworthy risk to the life of children's. Be that as it may, absence of appropriate regulatory usage of the different plans, authoritative and protected decrees constitute as a noteworthy risk for the expansion of the life and freedom of children's as subjects of the general public. A great many children's in this day and age experience the most noticeably awful types of children work which includes Child prostitution, Child Slavery, Child Trafficking, and Child Soldiers. In this cutting edge period of material and innovative progression, children's in relatively every nation are by and large unfeelingly abused.

In India Problem and Prospectus of Children

1. **Child Labour Issue:** Child Labour has turned into a major issue in India. It is no uncertainty, a financial issue. A national study had demonstrated that in excess of 16 million children's between eight to fourteen are to a great scope selected in lodgings and motel, in coffeehouses, eateries, in business firms, in plants and fisheries. They are locked in into a wide range of work for gaining something for the family. Subsequently, they are additionally denied of essential instruction, without which possibility of achievement in life is remote. Children's are utilized in farming work; they drive trucks and deal with dairy cattle. Young lady children's need to go about as house keeper workers and sitters. They cook and clean, they wash garments and gather fuel. The reality of the matter is that various laws have been forced to anticipate children work. In any case, they are more mocked than complied. The boycott has been forced to spare the children's from dangerous works and to re-establish their joyful adolescence. In any case, some opines that if the boycott is forced without the courses of action of appropriate restoration of the children labourers, it would be of no impact. There is no state which is free from the

shrewdness of children work.The scourge of children work isn't preceded to India alone. It has broadly spread to such creating nations as Nepal, Pakistan, Bangladesh, Burma and Sri Lanka.Destitution isn't the main factor in charge of children's are being locked in as work. They came less expensive and their folks don't have work openings. Fitting government disability measures ought to be received for guaranteeing the sanctioning of the law. Indian Government must approach to evacuate this revile with sufficient money related help to the poor family. The Government must orchestrate free training and treatment for the children's. Children Labour Act must be appropriately kept up and taken after.

2. **Enforcement of Anti-Child Labour Laws:** Laws to be upheld with the heartbeat of society, a business who abuses the tyke by giving extremely least sum than the fundamental pay, ought to be punished and rebuffed. Key rights to each tyke article 21 A, free and mandatory instruction to all children's between 8-14 years old, this ought to be execution in the public eye as indicated by above standards, there ought to be social equity towards the children at bring down strata

3. **Child Trafficking:** Abolitionist subjection activists say a large number of children are disappearing from some of India's remote ancestral territories as human traffickers react to a surge popular for residential tyke work in blasting urban locale. In the vicinity of 2011 and 2013, in excess of 10,500 children were enrolled as absent from the focal territory of Chhattisgarh, one of India's poorest states. The larger part is accepted to have been trafficked out of the state and into residential work or different

types of children work in urban areas. "Trafficking for sex and different purposes has dependably existed in India, however trafficking children's for residential servitude is a moderately new advancement," says HS Phoolka, a senior backer at India's incomparable court and a human rights legal advisor and dissident. "This is because of rising interest for local cleaning specialists because of rising wage in urban zones and wide scale neediness in provincial zones. This trafficking demonstrates the ascent of gigantic imbalance in India." The missing children's in Chhattisgarh speak to a little level of the evaluated 135,000 children accepted to be trafficked in India consistently. However the rate at which they are disappearing from remote towns in the south of the state is causing caution. The nature and scope of trafficking range from mechanical and household work, to constrained early relational unions and business sexual misuse. Existing investigations demonstrate that more than 40 for each penny of girls sex specialists go into prostitution before the age of 18 years. In addition, for youngsters who have been trafficked and saved, open doors for recovery stays rare and reintegration process exhausting. The most exceedingly bad sufferer among working youngsters are the individuals who are utilized for family work and regularly alluded as tyke household specialists (CDWs). For quite a while, the official offices in charge of security of youngsters denied their reality. Our constitution denies human trafficking and progressive governments have defined laws proposed to handle it, with the essential administrative instrument being the Corrupt Traffic (Prevention) Act 1956, however these laws are either powerless or insufficiently authorized.

Youngsters' powerlessness and presentation to infringement of their rights stays across the board and different in nature. In any case, the genuine reason for stress is UNIFEM's report which says s that 40 % of India's cops are ignorant of children trafficking issue. However because of consistent battle by the NGOs upheld by global offices, now the Government has restricted work of children' beneath 14 years as residential assistance from tenth October 2006.It is accounted for that in Metropolitan urban areas like Mumbai, Kolkata, Delhi and Chennai greater part of local help are children especially young girls underneath 14 years.

4. Health Hazards Faced by Children in Indian Society

a. **Infant Mortality:** Infant child mortality is as high as 63 deaths for every 1,000 live births. Most infant death happens in the primary month of life; up to 47 for every penny in the principal week itself. While the Infant Mortality Rate demonstrated a quick decay amid the 1980s, the abatement has moderated amid the previous decade. Maternal death are comparably high , The explanations behind this high mortality are that couple of ladies approach gifted birth specialists less still to quality crisis obstetric care. Likewise, just 15 for every penny of moms get finish antenatal care also, just 58 for every penny get iron or folate tablets or syrup.

b. **HIV/AIDS Faced by Children:** It is estimated 220,000 children infected by HIV/AIDS and 55,000 to 60,000 children are born every year to mothers who are HIV positive. Without treatment, these newborns stand an estimated 30% chance of becoming infected during the mother's pregnancy, labour or through breastfeeding after six months. There is effective treatment available, but this is not reaching all women and children who need it. The mobilization and greater involvement of NGOs in programmes for the development of children and women has increased the potential to accelerate the development process in achieving the national goals for children.

5.   Solution for the Health Issues Faced in India

a.   Social services schemes should be adopted, there has to be contact points to help children and families survive crises, such as disease, or loss of home and shelter

b.   Family sensitized over control of fertility so that families are not burdened by children

c.   Awareness among children and parents about the importance of healthy life preaching in small or big crusades.

d.   Making children to join the vocational training centres, which should be easily accessible. It will be a powerful, tool to assist children in escaping the poverty trap.

6.   Laws Framed in Indian Constitution: The constitution of India prohibits every kind of discrimination of individuals, including children. The major provisions of rights thatare relating to the rights of children are follows:

a.   Article 14 recognizes the equal rights. It empowers the State to make special provisions for the development of women and children.

b. Article 19 confers freedom of speech, expression, to reside any part of the country, and move freely which is guaranteed equally to every child.

c. Article 21 guarantees free life and liberty, and make it obligatory that free and compulsory education be provided to every child in the age group of six to fourteen years.

d. Article 23 prohibits traffic in human beings and abolishes bonded labour which includes women and children of our country.

e. Article 24 bans the employment or recruitment of children below 14 years in any factory or mine or heavy and harmful industries to the health and growth of children.

Role of National Commission for Protection of Child Rights

As per numerous reports of worldwide offices and non-administrative associations, India is the significant nation contrasted with a considerable lot of the immature nations including the African district, where in the predicament of children is more regrettable in making the most of their rights as subjects of the State. The fundamental reason is the wastefulness of the authoritative wings of the state to legitimately actualize and screen the circumstance, aside from destitution, which is another noteworthy factor that denies the privileges of children. The National Commission for Protection of Child Rights (NCPCR) was set up in March 2007 under the Commission for Protection of Child Rights Act, 2005. As indicated by the arrangements of the Act, a tyke is characterized as a man underneath the age of 18 years on the lines of the United Nations Child Rights Convention definition. The Commission's Mandate is to guarantee that all Laws, Policies, Programs, and Administrative Mechanisms are in consonance with the Child Rights viewpoint as revered in the Constitution of India and the UN Convention on the Rights of the Child. The commission has the energy of common court in guaranteeing their obligations and duties towards children.

Conclusion

Since Independence, until today, the constitution of India and the States embraced various plans for the advancement and welfare of children's. It has built up various breakthroughs broadly and universally to release its sacred and worldwide commitments in advancing the best advantages of children's. Be that as it may, because of expanding populace, destitution and so on a huge number of children's are not in a situation to have a fulfilled dinner once in a day. Further, the antagonistic sex proportion of female populace is a reason for concern. Aside from the state and a couple of non-administrative associations, the general population of the nation likewise need to release their bit of administrations for the expansion of the youngsters' rights is vital. We the general population of the nation promise to endeavour hard to stretch out their assistance to one of the defenceless and most affected crowded of the nation, specifically children's, the future ages of the nation with a specific end goal to wipe out each remove that originates from the eyes children's. Be that as it may, here we recommend a few measures to be executed for the bigger welfare of our general public and to see the youth back to our children's.

References

1. Ansari, P.A. 2016. *"Rights of Children in India: Problems and Prospectus"*. International Journal of Innovative Research and Development, ISSN 2278-0211, Vol-5, Issue-6, pp. 48-52

2. Bhat, B.A. 2010. *"Human rights perspective and legal framework of child labour with special reference to India"*. International Journal of Sociology and Anthropology, ISSN 2006-988x, Vol.-2, Issue-2, pp.019-022.

3. Goonesekere, Savitri. 2008. *"Children, Law and Justice: A South Asian Perspective"*. SAGE Publication, New Delhi.

4. Report of Training Workshop on Rights of the Child, University of Kerala, 2010.

5. Sen, Munira., Madhyam. 2010. *"Child Trafficking"* Bangalore, India.

6. Srivastava, Ravi and Sasikumar, S.K. 2003. *"An Overview of Migration in India, its aim and Key Issues"* paper presented at the Regional Conference on Migration,

7. UNICEF 2000. *First Call for Children: World Declaration and Plan of Action from the World Summit for Children*, Convention on the Rights of the Child. New York: UNICEF.

8. UNICEF 2004. *The State of the World's Children 2004*. New York: UNICEF. pp. 7

CHAPTER

8

PROBLEM AND PROSPECTUS OF WOMEN RIGHTS IN INDIA

Meenu Tanwar
Associate Professor & Head
Department of Sociology,
Ch. Ballu Ram Godara Govt. Girls P.G. College,
Sri Ganganagar
(Rajasthan)

Introduction

Women developed as a particular intrigue aggregate in the nineteenth century essentially in light of the fact that the bourgeoisie equitable unrests of seventeenth and eighteenth century that rejected women from their idea of equity. This refinement depended on sexual orientation. From that point forward women as a cooperative had pursued battle for acknowledgment of their rights as an individual. Women' execute multilateral part in the general public i.e. as a provider of her family, as a care taker of her family as a mother, spouse, girl and specialist organization to the general public. Despite the way that the women' commitment to the nation's improvement is equivalent to that of their male partner, still they encounter various confinements that limit them from grasping their potential for development. It was against this foundation that the administration's everywhere throughout the world wanted to organize the interests of women and their support at each phase of the advancement procedure. Women as a centre gathering of concern rose as a noteworthy subject in the Millennium Development Objective. The Millennium Development Goal are the eight objectives set by the United Nations in 2000 which will go about as measuring stick to decide the progression toward the devastation of worldwide neediness. UN expressed that 'Sexual orientation Equality and Women Empowerment' as one of the Millennium Development Goals to be achieved by the year 2015. The term Women's strengthening suggests the capacity of the women take all the essential choices autonomously identified with her for the duration of her life expectancy that will guarantee her achievement in all parts of life. However these objectives are a long way from being in a nation like India. Infect frequently women in India are denied of their essential ideal to respect additionally take off alone the topic of sexual orientation equity. The present paper investigates the inquiries integral on women right side in India that is on a very basic level man centric in nature. The article endeavours to ponder the few difficulties looked by the women in India like the settlement, female foeticide, refusal of legacy, deal and trafficking of girls and so forth. The target of the paper is to advance procedures to engage women who are as people as men may be.

Violation of Women Rights in Past

It has been over and over said nowadays that women in India are appreciating the rights equivalent to men. Be that as it may, as a general rule, the women in India have been the sufferers from past. In prior circumstances as well as, women need to confront segregation, unfairness and shame. Give us now a chance to examine the violations done against the women despite being given rights equivalent to men. These focuses will clarify that proceeds with infringement of human privileges of women in India. The Indian women misuse isn't the present marvel. Or maybe she is being misused from the early circumstances. The women in Indian culture never remained for a reasonable status. The accompanying violations were done against the women in the past circumstances.

1. **Devdasis:** Devadasis was a religious practice in a few sections of southern India, in which women were hitched to a divinity or sanctuary. In the later period, the ill-conceived sexual misuse of the devadasi's turned into a standard in some piece of the nation.

2. **Sati:** Despite the fact that Sati, an activity whereupon the activity of setting dowagers on the funeral service fires of their life partner, was banned in the pre pioneer India by social reformer Raja Rammohan Roy, however this training kept on winning in post pilgrim India. The talk on sati was empowered in the post autonomy India in 1986 when a youthful lady from Rajasthan named Roop Kanwar was determined to the fire of her better half. As an outcome in 1987, the Sati Prevention Act was passed which announced the act of sati a wrongdoing

for which capital punishment can likewise be given to the culprits of such wrongdoing. The demonstration likewise proclaimed that the 'glorification' of sati by raising a sanctuary and revering of the expired women as a divine being is additionally denied. However certain area of individuals sees this law as obstruction in their entitlement to practice manages of their religion.

3. **Early Child Marriage:** In India in spite of the fact that there exist a law notwithstanding the relational unions of children's at crude age, yet it is as yet being polished in various parts of India. Chid Marriage Act 2006 denies children marriage and proclaims 18 years and 21 years as the marriageable age for the girls and boys. As per the National Population Policy, "more than half of the girls wed underneath the age of 18, bringing about a commonplace regenerative example of 'too soon, excessively visit, too much', bringing about a high IMR5." Child marriage detracts from a girl children the purity of her developmental years of life vital for physical, passionate and mental advancement. Spousal brutality particularly sexual savagery executed by spouses has serious impact on the pure personality and body of the child. Indeed, even today in India some of children' are offered on the promising day of Akas Teej in Rajasthan.

4. **Female Foeticide:** The low status of women goes ahead with the act of child murder, foeticide, sex-specific foetus removal which has turned out to be normal because of the amniocentesis innovation, and mal-food among girl children's. In India it is assessed that around "10 million female babies have been prematurely ended over the most recent 20 years". "The child sex

proportion in Punjab declined from 894 out of 1961 to 793 of every 2001. In Haryana, the children sex proportion plunged from 910 of every 1961 to 820 out of 2018." despite the way that the Government of India have announced pre-birth sex assurance using amniocentesis as unlawful, still Illicit end of female hatchlings by untrained medical caretakers and staff is broadly predominant especially in Northern conditions of India like Haryana, Rajasthan and Punjab. All these have brought about the acceleration of maternal death rate.

5. **Forced Evictions and Exclusion:** In India regularly the dowagers are expelled from their marital home and are allowed to sit unbothered to sustain themselves and their children following the end of their life partners. The UN Special Reporter on Adequate Housing contends: "In all nations, regardless of whether 'created' or 'creating', legitimate security of residency for women is completely reliant on the men they are related with. Women headed family units and women by and large are far less secure than men. Not very many women claim arrive. An isolated or separated from lady with no land and a family to nurture frequently winds up in an urban ghetto, where her security of residency is, best case scenario faulty". "There is expanding securing proof that, in poor families, women spend more on essential family needs, while men spend a huge part on individual products, for example, liquor, tobacco, and so forth".

6. **Societal Violence against Women:** The community and social orders in India in a large portion of the spots are

bound up with man centric regularizing universe from which women could scarcely get genuine equity. The religious groups, town groups or the counterfeit groups like proficient bodies are not really encapsulation of correspondence amongst men and women. Regularly the religious groups have made the life of the women more terrible by compelling them to embrace preservationist practices that are hurtful to women.

Indian Constitutions Women's Right for Protection

The constitution of India presents unique rights upon women. The constitution producers were very much aware of the subordinate and in reverse position of women in the general public. They tried a few endeavours for inspire of women in our general public. The state is coordinated to accommodate maternity alleviation to female labourers under Article 42 of the Constitution, while Article 51-A proclaims it as a crucial obligation of each Indian national to repudiate hones to regard the nobility of women. Indian Parliament has passed the Protection of Human Rights Act, 1993 for the best possible execution of Article 51-A. Indian Parliament throughout the years have made critical strides for through enactments to accomplish the objective of engaging the women in India. The noteworthy among them are the Equal Remuneration Act, the Prevention of Immoral Traffic Act, the Sati Prevention Act, and the Dowry Prohibition Act and so on. Separated from these, the 73rd and 74th Constitution Acts accommodated 33% booking for women in both pachayat and Nagar palika foundations and in addition for the places of chairpersons of these bodies. These two revisions expelled the bottlenecks from the ways of women strengthening at the neighbourhood level. Truth is told it has been discovered that the Karnataka sends greatest number of women to the PRIs took after by Kerala and Manipur. Keeping in mind the end goal to encourage rise to cooperation of women at the national and state level governmental issues, the bill accommodating 33% reservation of seats for women in national and States lawmaking bodies has been presented in Parliament. Other than this, the legislature in India have instituted an assortment of laws like Dowry Prohibition Act, Sati counteractive action Act and so forth to ensure the privileges of the women.

Conclusion

Therefore to put it plainly, the Millennium Development Goal on sex equity and women' strengthening can be acknowledged in India just when the customary practices like female child murder, share passings, respect killings by khap panchayats, abusive behaviour at home, or sexual manhandle is dispensed with. It is at exactly that point that sexual orientation balance and women' strengthening can turn into a reality.

References

1. Bhattacharya S, Pratinidhi K.A. 1994. "A community based study of infertile women from urban slum". *Indian J Matern Child Health*. Vol.-5, Issue-15, pp.6.

2. Dhanoa, Ritu. 2012. "Violation of Women Human Rights in India". *Shiv Shakti International Journal in Multidisciplinary and Academic Research'*, ISSN 2278-5973, Vol-1, Issue-4, pp. 1-9.

3. Ganatra, B.R., Coyaji, K.J., and Rao, V.N. 1996. *"EM Hospital Research Centre*; 1996"*. Community Cum Hospital Based Case-Control Study on Maternal Mortality: A Final Report.

4. Kishwar, Madhu. 1999. *"Off the beaten Track: Rethinking Gender Justice for Indian Women"*. OUP, New Delhi, pp. 200-205.

5. National Commission on Population, National Population Policy 2000-Objectives, National Commission on Population, Government of India.

6. Saryal, Sutapa. 2014. "Women Rights in India-Problems and Prospectus". *International Journal of Social Science*, ISSN 2319-3565,Vol-3, Issue-7, pp.49-53.

7. Shashi and Krishan. 2008. "Indian Democracy and Women's Human Rights". *Journal of Social Sciences.*

CHAPTER 9

WOMEN EMPOWERMENT AND HUMAN RIGHTS

Balveer Singh Verma
Assistant Professor
Satyam College for Girls
Sayadwala,
Abohar
(Punjab)

Introduction

Simply stated, a right is a claim of a individual recognized by the society and the state obviously a proper definition of the tern right has three ingredients. First, it is a claim of the individual, second individual should receive recognition by the community and finally political recognition. Rights are just like moral declarations unless they are protected by the state.

The rights have a moral character whether Human rights. Natural rights political, economic, social moral and social, moral and civil rights, in other words, they are the rights which a society properly organized on the basis of good will should recognize. And rights are not only related to social welfare, they also related to a dynamic character.

According to H.J. Laski. "Rights, in fact, are those conditions of social life without which no man can seek, in general, to be himself at his best. For since the state exists it make possible that achievement, it is only by maintaining rights that its end may be secured".

According to Gilchrist

"Rights arise, therefore, from individuals as members of society, and from the recognition that, for society there is ultimate good which may be reached by the development of the power inherent in every individual". So in this way they are the rights which a society organized on the basis of good will should recognize.

However, the most important point, which was highlights the "Humanism and also Human rights: that is, according to Marxism as Well as New leftism, seems new society in which man has a free happy and dignified life, Marx termed it there of human emancipation"man is free all sorts of exploitation and oppression, Glorious human values prevail.

Human Rights

A modified version of natural rights and civil rights, which are coupled with each other, and has assumed a significance of its own ever since the formulation of the Universal Declaration of Human Rights by the Human Rights commission and their adoption by the General Assembly of the United Nations in 1948. Elinoar Ruzwert, the president of

United Nations General Assembly, declared that instead of "Rights of man, She declared as Human Rights" in 1948, so that, 'women rights' or 'women' were included in this declaration.

Now -a- days, human rights are become more important and giving more importance to them because from the grass root level, it means family level to International level every aspect which is related to development, security, welfare of the people etc., related to human rights or comes under human rights moreover any decision which was taken and which is taking by the governments of any nation is related to human rights, The human rights are depend on basic rule of "All are equal, no discrimination" this is the aim of human rights.

Human rights that are applying to all human beings therefore human rights are universal, all human beings come under human rights and holders of human rights without any discrimination, every human being has their rights, and these rights protect especially human existence.

In this regard, one can recognize a positive tendency of acceptance of human rights by states, a growth of an international institutionalization for the protection of human rights and a progress of the mechanisms for monitoring human rights performances by states to respect the Universality of human rights and some small steps by the corporate world.

Because human rights establish moral boundaries so, Human rights do not shop before fractions, cultures, etc.

Status of Women

Traditional Indian literature gave high respect to women e.g. in Vedic period women leads equal status with men. Manu had said"where women are honored, the Gods are pleased but where they are not, no sacred rite yields any reward".

Yagnavalkya said, "Women are the embodiment of all divine virtues on earth and the Ramayana and Mahabharata gives full credit to women". After that, slowly women were treated by barbarous customs like "Sati" [burning of widow on the funeral pyre of her husband denial of right to remarry to widows, female infanticide, existence of "devadasi" system, child marriages, etc., Women suffered from lots of disabilities. Women is psychologically felt inferior to men, physically women is dubbed as dull and dud, intellectually no wisdom and socially, women has a place lower than man, she is made to lead second class citizenship or subordinate life, women is considered ineligible for all public life, they confine to four walls, or family -mothering the babies, even in family life, they always secondary, these are all caused by man's domination or atrocities and the main weakness point of women is physically they are very weaker than men. Almost half of the women population dependent always at one, or the other time, on man, be, he a father, husband or the son, yet the women, today is no more a commodity to be bought and sold at man's whims.

Over the years, the women movement has developed a theory of power of society which sees the relationship between the sexes as one of in equality subordination and oppression and which sees this as a problem of political power than a fact of nature. Feminist regard the distinction between men and women not merely biological, but also sociological and thereafter political, men and women are biologically different, but they are seen, regarded and structured socially as different gender, The masculine gender, being physically strong and having made himself as the in charge of the external or what may be called public, exploits woman by considering her as an inferior being, a slave, and commodity.

In Indian culture women are subjected to gender discrimination right from the births. The female infanticide is widely prevalent even though it is highly in practice; an estimated 1.2 million lives were snuffed out either through abortion or post natal murders. The girls are also allowed to remain under nourished and, therefore, the female mortality rate is much higher than that of boys. Girl children are denied the proper educational facilities, nourishment and medical facilities. Parents and other family members think that they are burden to the family.

The gender bias not only reflected on one aspect, it society reflects on political, social, economic each and every point in the society reflects by the gender bias, even in jobs also it shows impact. In many places of India and worldwide, women are denied job opportunities, because the men folk more equipped to the job, and they feel that for women right place is kitchen and rearing children. Women also have to face sexual harassment, and the position of dalit women is so worst these are all live example to discrimination which was facing by women folk.

In political aspect, while the women's vote in terms of numbers is not much behind that of the men, their representation in legislative bodies has been very poor. The highest representation of Loksabha was in 1984 and that too eight percent and all over the India the State Assemblies also have a meager representation from women folk, so, women are slowly alienated from the political system.

Not surprising women are used like surrogates to their men folk be-cause after introducing 73'd Amendment Act in 1992, according to this Act 1/3 seats reserved for women, so reserved quota would be filled by the wives, daughters, etc, relations, women's representations in political field, and decision making bodies is very low.

There have many social legislations designed to achieve betterment of women, but they remain as paper tigers, rarely to be followed. In present times, the number of women either government or private offices is increasingly tremendously but compare to women population it is very low, And it will be wrong to state that as a result of all these efforts all the women in India have emancipated.

Still the male domination of the society was a fact. And women were suffering immense social envious and social oppression within the family, and also in the society. They were also suffering from illiteracy, ignorance, and economically dependent position etc. Polygamy was in practice still it is continuing, women not even the right to divorce (just like a curse.)

In this context the Indian constellation included human rights in the fundamental rights to protect every individual right, and for the protection of human rights so many provisions existed by the Indian constitution. In the same way, in 1993 the Indian government established Human rights commissions at both central and state level to strength-en the human rights and proper implementation.

In India, even though a largest democratic country suffering from human rights problems. Like children, women, etc., so many long lasting problems are here E.g.: 'women issue' is a chronic problem, so many number of rape cases are reading in every day news papers even 4 years children also victimized to this cruel behaviour, still unashamed violations of human rights are took place in all parts of the world especially with chronic problems. In this way number of international and regional instruments has drawn attention to Women human rights issues.

UN convention on the Elimination of All Forms of Discrimination against women adopted in 1979, and after eight year CEDAW came into force. CEDAW noted as, The International Bill of Rights for Women. In addition, required proper safe guards for their realization, be-cause conferment of rights is not enough or sufficient.

It is essential that governments should protect and promote people's rights moreover protection of rights, it is not only duty of governments similarly, and people also must be vigilant. Therefore, it is the proud spirit of citizens, less than the letter of the law, which is their most real safeguard.

In 1993, 45years after the Universal Declaration of Human Rights was adopted, and the UN world conference on Human Rights in Vienna confirmed that women rights were human rights.

And if anyone or anywhere, in identifying neglect of women's rights as human rights violation and in drawing attention to the relationship between gender and human rights violations should be punished. And this was a step forward in recognizing the rightful claims of women folk who were sharing half of the humanity.

The CEDAW defines the right of women to be free from all forms of Discrimination and also look action to protect this right. Under CE-DAW look many actions to protect women's rights such as prepared one agenda for national action to end discrimination, for achieving equality between men and women for equal access, equal opportunities in all the fields such as education, health, employment etc., introduced core principles. So CEDAW is the only human rights treaty which has creates a new world for women and women's rights.

In 1994, the International Conference on Population and Development in Cairo (ICPD) articulated and affirmed the relationship between advancement and fulfillment of rights and gender equality and equity. The ICPD declared in their programme of action that, the achievement of sustainable development depends on women empowerment and political social, economic improvement, so ICPD recognized that, the highly important and essential of women empowerment.

In 1995, the fourth world conference on women in Beijing discussed in wider range on women's rights and the gender equality, women's empowerment as one of the eight Millennium Development goals. But many promises have not yet to be kept.

Conclusion

Women are suffering low socio- economic, political inequalities over the past decade, and women empowerment is a new challenge for all and still women getting less money than men, even same kind of work, Gender based violence (never ending) increasing of trafficking on women etc., these are all for instance of women condition at worldwide.

The commission EDAM trying to identify emerging trends, injustice, discriminatory practices against women for the purposes of formulation of right and useful policies, and initiate development strategies to protect women's human rights as well as gender equality.

When social, economic, political emancipation is possible and healthy development of democratic process free from corruption and free from criminalization of politics took place in the society when women's political participations is possible for women empowerment and emancipation.

References

1.	Awasthy, SS. Indian Government and politics, pp. 408

2.	Awasthy, S.S. Indian Government and politics, pp. 409

3.	Awasthy, S.S. Indian Government and politics, pp. 411

4.	Awasthy, S.S. Indian Government and politics, pp. 410

5.	Johari, J.C. Contemporary Political Theory, pp. 229.

6.	Johari, L.C. Contemporary Political Theory, pp. 657.

7.	Laski, OP, cit., pp. 89.

8.   Peter, K.C. Human Rights Education, University of Teacher Education of Central Switzerland.

CHAPTER
10

HUMAN RIGHTS AND GENDER EQUALITY: THE UNALIENABLE APPANAGE

Dr. Manvendra Singh
Assistant Professor,
Department of Government and Public Administration,
School of Social Sciences and Languages,
Lovely Professional University,
Phagwara. (Punjab)

Introduction

The problem of Human Rights has been a raging fire for decades on end. With this is linked the problem of gender justice for women's emancipation. The pity is that much though we talk of human rights, the fact remains that the word 'Human' took long to be defined and understood by the human activists. Human rights are "commonly understood as inalienable fundamental rights to which a person is inherently entitled because she or he is a human being."[1] It is unfortunate that the problem of human rights was on the anvil and activists were added to codify some of these rights. A committee was formed by the United Nations, headed by

Mrs. Eleanor Roosevelt to prepare a draft of human rights. What a pity that even a committee headed by a woman came out with a statement that all men are brothers and when subsequently Eleanor Roosevelt was quizzed by media mavens, how is it that being a lady she could not do anything for the women, her answer was that men included women also. This is very unfortunate that for a long time men have been using this alibi to bypass women in a clever and subtle manner and even Mrs. Roosevelt felt into this trap late by male enthusiasts. It took many years by the United Nations and a good deal of effort to redress this wrong. The word 'men' was substituted by human beings, thereby, indicating by implication that even women are entitled to certain rights as being human.

The question of human rights was never taken seriously till the two World Wars. Even before these wars, many wars have taken place but they were addressed as national wars involving combatants and belligerents from various nations. This was the first time that the canvas of the theatre of war widened phenomenally to become global and hence the last two big wars were declared World wars. Apart from the huge areal spread that these two wars covered, the magnitude of disaster was unprecedented. This is mainly because this was the first time when the civilian population and civilian property was destroyed in the war badly. Cities were bombarded, thereby killing a vast number of unarmed civilians including women, children, old and the infirm. The scale of bombardment being too big destroyed not only military installations but also civilian settlements, thereby causing huge collateral damage to property.

The bombardment at Hiroshima and Nagasaki in Japan was

an eye opener for the simple reason that the victims of disaster were mostly the unarmed and innocent civilian population. The after effects of the bombardment were terrible. Those who were killed were considered fortunate to have lost their lives in one fall stroke. However, the pity was that those who survived became human wretches and kept on dying many times. This added to the agony and pain of this disastrous human conflagration. Incidentally, it was this magnitude of tragedy that awakened human consciousness and eventually people came out with the chants of human rights.

The League of Nations was formed in 1919 as a result of the Paris Peace Conference and the Treaty of Versailles and the main objectives of this League were to prevent further war with the help of collective security measures, to encourage the member nations for disarmament, to help in the settlement of disputes amongst the countries with negotiation and diplomacy skills and thus, working diligently for the overall human welfare around the globe.

The difficulty with human rights is regards to an absence of agreed definition on what constitutes human beings. The word 'human being' is being bandied about with gay abandon by the protagonists of status quo in all countries which are guilty of discrimination and apartheid policies. These people maintain that the precise treatment which they accord to a section of their population is an internal matter of their country and, therefore, it is beyond the jurisdiction of any internal organization or tribunal. As a result of this insensitive policy, ethnic minorities continue to suffer trials and tribulations and face acts of human barbarity. For long, the apartheid regime of South Africa refused to abide by the

United Nations declarations and was even willing to face international sanctions but would not give up its discriminatory policies. This happens not only in the countries that practise colour bar but even in normal countries having an ethnic divide and differences.The fratricidal civil war of extermination that was perpetuated owing to inter-ethnic jealousy in a predominantly black country like Sudan, which divided the nation into two parts i.e. the North Sudan and the South Sudan, is an instance in point of discrimination being perpetuated even in spite of the two groups having the same colour of their skin.[2]

In the famous Yalta Conference (also known as the Crimea Conference) held in 1945, the Allied Powers including the United States of America, Great Britain and the Soviet Union were agreed to create a new body to succeed the League's role in the form of the United Nations. Since its inception, the U.N has played a significant role in promoting the international human rights awareness and laws. The provisions of the United Nations Charter provided a basis for the development of international human rights protection.[3]

Classification of Human Rights

There are a number of different ways in which human rights can be categorized and classified but the most common categorization at the international level has been to divide them into Civil and Political Rights on one hand and Economic, Social and Cultural Rights on the other. The various civil and political rights and the economic, social and cultural rights were protected in articles 3 to 21 and articles 22 to 28 of the Universal Declaration of Human Rights (UDHR) and in the International Covenant on Civil and

Political Rights (ICCPR) respectively. These taxonomies of human rights are indivisible. It was even validated by the International Covenant on Civil and Political Rights and the International Covenant on Economic, Social and Cultural Rights, 1966 and the Vienna Declaration. Later, these views were again endorsed in the World Summit in New York in 2005.

Universal Declaration of Human Rights

The Universal Declaration of Human Rights was adopted by the United Nations General Assembly on 10th December, 1948 in Paris, France.[4] It was the result of Second World War aftermath on humanity. With the end of this war and the birth of the United Nations, the international community joined hands together and vowed that they will not allow the atrocities that happened during the World War period ever again. World leaders decided to complement the UN Charter with a road map to guarantee the rights of each and every individual across the globe. The Universal Declaration of Human Rights was framed by member of the international human rights commission with the former first lady Eleanor Roosevelt being the chairperson who began to discuss an international bill of rights in 1947. A Canadian legal scholar, jurist, and human rights advocate John Peters Humphrey and a French professor and judge, Rene Samuel Cassin, were responsible for giving the shape to this Universal Declaration of Human Rights document.[5] Few of the provisions and clauses in the Universal Declaration of Human Rights document were researched and written by a committee of international experts on legal issues, human rights and it included representatives and members from across the world with leaders such as Mahatma Gandhi etc.

International Treaties

The International Covenant on Civil and Political Rights and the International Covenant on Economic, Social and Cultural Rights were adopted by the United Nations in 1966 and were binding on all states that have signed this treaty. Since then, various accords and pacts have been presented at the global level. These agreements are known as *Human Rights Instruments.* Some of the most important conventions are as follows:

a.   Convention on the Elimination of All Forms of Discrimination against Women

b.   United Nations Convention against Torture

c.   Convention on the Rights of Persons with Disabilities

d.   Convention on the Elimination of All Forms of Racial Discrimination

e.   International Convention on the Protection of the Rights of All Migrant Workers and Member of their Families

f.   Convention on the Rights of the Child

Apart from the protection by these international treaties and instruments, there is a provision of *Customary International Law* i.e. those aspects of international law that derive from Custom and tradition. Along with general principles of law and treaties, customary international law is considered by the International Court of Justice, Jurists, the United Nations and its members to be among the primary sources of the international law. The International Court of Justice Statute defines customary international law in Article 38 (1) (b) as, "evidence of a general practice accepted as law."[6] Most of the times, it would be determined through two main factors, the general practice of states and what states have accepted as law.[7]

International Humanitarian Law

International Humanitarian Law is also known as the Law of Armed Conflict and it deals with the law that regulates and controls the conduct of armed conflicts (*jus in bello*). It is that branch of international law which seeks to limit the effects of armed conflicts by protecting persons who are not or no longer participating in hostilities and by restricting and regulating the means and methods of warfare available to combatants. It is inspired by considerations of humanity and the mitigation of human suffering. Serious violations of international humanitarian law are called war crimes. International humanitarian law, *jus in bello*, regulates the conduct of forces when engaged in war or armed conflict. It is distinct from *jus ad bellum* which regulates the conduct of engaging in war or armed conflict and includes crimes against peace and of war of aggression. Together the *jus in bello* and *jus ad bellum* comprise the two strands of the laws of war governing all aspects of international armed conflicts.

The law is mandatory for nations bound by the appropriate treaties. There are also other customary unwritten rules of war, many of which were explored at the Nuremberg War Trials. By extension, they also define both the *permissive* rights of these powers as well as *prohibitions* on their conduct when dealing with irregular forces and non-signatories.

International humanitarian law operates on a strict division between rules applicable in international armed conflict and those relevant to armed conflicts not of an international nature. This dichotomy is very much criticized.[8]

Geneva Conventions

The Geneva Conventions were the result of a process that was developed in various stages between 1864 and 1949. These conventions came into existence owing to the efforts by Henry Dunant, a Swiss businessman and social activist. During a business trip in 1859 he witnessed the aftermath of the Battle of Solferino (in the modern day Italy). He later recorded his memories and experiences in the book *"A Memory of Solferino"* which inspired him to create the International Committee of the Red Cross in 1863. The Geneva Conventions were focussed on the protection of civilians and those who can no longer fight in an armed conflict. As a consequence of World War II, all four conventions were revised based on previous revisions and some on the basis of the 1907 Hague Conventions, and readopted by the international community in 1949. Later conferences have added provisions prohibiting certain methods of warfare and addressing issues of civil wars. The first three Geneva Conventions were revised, expanded, and replaced, and the fourth one was added, in 1949.

- The Geneva Convention *for the Amelioration of the Condition of the Wounded and Sick in Armed Forces in the Field* was adopted in 1864. It was significantly revised and replaced by the 1906 version, the 1929 version, and later the First Geneva Convention of 1949.

- The Geneva Convention *for the Amelioration of the*

Condition of Wounded, Sick and Shipwrecked Members of Armed Forces at Sea was adopted in 1906.[9] It was significantly revised and replaced by the Second Geneva Convention of 1949.

- The Geneva Convention *relative to the Treatment of Prisoners of War* was adopted in 1929. It was significantly revised and replaced by the Third Geneva Convention of 1949.

- The Fourth Geneva Convention *relative to the Protection of Civilian Persons in Time of War* was adopted in 1949.

The Geneva Conventions of 1949 may be seen, therefore, as the result of a process which began in 1864. Today they have "achieved universal participation with 194 parties." This means that they apply to almost any international armed conflict.[10] The Additional Protocols, however, have yet to achieve near-universal acceptance, since the United States and several other significant military powers (like Iran, Israel, India and Pakistan) are currently not parties to them.[11]

United Nations Human Rights Council

It is an inter-governmental body within the United Nations System *per se* and is the successor to the United Nations Commission on Human Rights. It is a subsidiary body of the United Nations General Assembly. It was created at the 2005 World Summit and has a mandate to investigate the violations of human rights.[12] The Human Rights Council may request the UN Security Council to take action when human rights violations occur. This action may be in the form of direct actions, may involve sanctions, and the UN Security Council may also refer cases to the International Criminal

Court (ICC) even if the issue being referred is outside the normal jurisdiction of the International Criminal Court.[13]

Role of Non-Governmental Organizations

The international non-governmental organizations such as Amnesty International, Human Rights Watch, International Service for Human Rights, International Federation for Human Rights, Oxfam etc. observe and monitor the human rights issues around the world and express their concerns, opinions and views on these topics. These NGOs have been said to "translate complex international issues into activities to be undertaken by concerned citizens in their own community."[14] These organizations are more often engaged in lobbying and advocating for the human rights issues and for demanding justice, liberty and equality for all.

Few Substantial International Human Rights

a. Right to Life: The right to life is a just and fair principle based on a belief that a human being has the right to live and survive and should not be unjustly killed by another human being. It is central while addressing the issues like euthanasia (the practice of intentionally ending a life in order to relieve pain and suffering), capital punishment, abortion, self defense and the morality of war and so on. Many human rights practitioners and activists around the world believes that sanctioning a death penalty to a person guilty for crime violates this very fundamental right to life.[15]

b. Freedom from Slavery: Slavery is that system under which people are treated as a mere property to be bought and sold and are forced to work for others.[16] Though it is officially illegal in majority of the countries yet there are still 20 to 30 million slaves worldwide.[17] It has existed in many cultures. Most of the slaves today are debt slaves, particularly in South Asian region and are under huge debt bondages incurred by lenders, sometimes even for generations. Human trafficking is primarily used for forcing women and children into sex industries.[18]

c. Freedom from Torture: It is the act of deliberately inflicting and causing severe physical or psychological pain and possible injury to a person or animal, usually to one who is physically restrained or otherwise under the torturer's control or custody and unable to defend them. Reasons for torture can include punishment, revenge, political re-education, deterrence, interrogation or coercion of the victim or a third party or simply the sadistic gratification of the torturer. Although torture was sanctioned by individuals, groups and nations throughout the history but in the 21[st]century, it is banned under international law and the domestic laws of many countries. It is considered to be a violation of human rights and is declared to be unacceptable by the Article 5 of the UN Universal Declaration of Human Rights, the Geneva Conventions of 1949 and few relevant additional protocols of 1977. But the fact remains that despite these international measures, torture, in some form or the other, is still practised by many states across the globe. A report by Amnesty International indicated that at least 81 percent world governments currently practise torture.[19]

d. Sexual orientation and gender identity: These rights are related with the free expression of gender identity and sexual orientation based on the right to respect for private life and the right not to be discriminated on the ground of "other status" as defined in various human rights conventions. It includes issues such as government recognition of same-sex relationships, Lesbian Gay Bisexual and Transgender (LGBT) rights, immigration equality, hate crime laws regarding violence against LGBT people, sodomy laws, anti-lesbianism laws, and equal age of consent for same sex activity and so on.

e. *Right to Water*: According to the United Nations Committee on Economic, Social and Cultural Rights, "the human right to water is indispensable for leading a life in human dignity. It is a prerequisite for the realization of other human rights." This marks a departure from the minutes of the 2nd World Water Forum in the Hague in 2000, which stated that water was a commodity to be bought and sold and it cannot be claim as a right.[20]

f. Right to Freedom of Thought, Conscience and Religion

g. Right to Freedom of Speech

h. Right to a Fair Trial

i. Right to Freedom of Movement

j. Right to Keep and Bear Arms

k. Right to Trade

l. Right to Internet Access and Digital rights

Gender Equality: An Indian Context

Gender equality means that men and women should be treated as equal and should not be discriminated on the basis of gender. It believes in challenging and even abolishing the age old social system of Patriarchy where the males are the primary authority figures in the society occupying and controlling the politics, property, resources, women and children etc. Females are generally subordinated to the males who have got all the privileges and perks. Power is generally held by the adult men.

The movement towards gender equality, especially in Western countries, began with the Suffragette movement of the late 19th century which allowed women to vote and to hold elected office. Later, in the 1960s, this issue of gender equality gained momentum with the ideas of women's liberation and feminism. Gradually, there have been significant changes in thinking levels and attitudes of the human societies around the world which resulted in the creation of more legislation for promoting gender justice. Providing gender equality is also one of the main goals of United Nations Millennium Project. According to it, "Every single Goal is directly related to women's rights, and societies where women are not afforded equal rights as men can never achieve development in a sustainable manner."[21]

The consistent degradation of women and social supremacy of men still prevails in India. Generally, women are viewed as a weaker gender, dowry burdens, and their social position is still considered as lower when compared with men and as a result, it has given birth to many socio-economic problems in this country. According to the Census 2011 figures, the sex ratio of India has reached from 933 women per 1000 men in 2001 to 940 women per 1000 men in 2011, showing a very marginal improvement. Only one state of India i.e. Kerela has managed to score fairly well where the sex ratio stood at 1058 women per 1000 men in 2001 and reached the new magical figure of 1084 women per 1000 men in 2011, thereby making it the only state with highest sex ratio. In 2011 Census figures, Haryana with 877 women per 1000 men has got the lowest sex ratio among states of India and Daman and Diu with 618 women per 1000 men has the lowest sex ratio among all the states and union territories of India. There is also a widespread gender disparity in the literacy rate in India. As per the Indian Census 2011 figures, the average literacy rate (age 7 and above) in India was 82.14% for men and 65.46% for women. The low female literacy rate has had a drastically negative influence on family planning and population stabilization efforts in India. In Western countries women are born not only with the political, economical and social rights and opportunities but also they have better health care facilities and according to a UN report, women in these countries live about six years longer than men. But the Indian scenario is quite different. In this country girls are being given less food and health care than boys, particularly in North India. Girls are breast fed for shorter periods, given less medical attention, fewer consultations and visits to a doctor and in case of an emergency either they are taken to hospital very late or not at all.[22] Female children are undernourished as compared to male children and they more often suffer from diseases like anaemia and malnourishment. Girls in India face higher risks of female foeticides, abortions, malnourishment, diseases, disabilities and retardation of growth and development. Their value to the family, state and nation has always been undervalued. And it is mainly because of the societal attitude and thinking towards the females over a long time. It is a common belief in India that "Bringing a girl child is like watering a plant in anothers' courtyard." Due to such beliefs she is often considered as a liability and a commodity. She is deprived of good food, education, opportunities and resources. The situation is worse in rural areas of India. According to a global study conducted by Thomson Reuters Corporation, a multinational media and information firm based in New York, USA, India is the 4th most dangerous country for a girl child in the world.[23]

Apart from this, women more often than not become the victims of violence inflicted upon them in the form of acid throwing, a premeditated crime intended to kill or maim the women permanently and to teach her a lesson. There are many cases of domestic violence and abuses against women and it has become a cause of concern for the government as well. According to a paper published in the *International Journal of Criminology and Sociological Theory* in 2007, there were 20,737 reported cases of rape, 8093 cases of death due to dowry, and 10,950 cases of sexual harassment with total crimes numbering to 1, 85,312. A United Nations Population Fund report claimed that up to 70 percent of married women in India aged between 15-49 are victims of beatings and coerced sex.

Eve teasing is also one of the major phenomenons that resulted in various assaults against women. It is generally reported in developing countries such as India, Pakistan and even Nepal. It is a form of sexual harassment or molestation of women by men. However, to prevent it, the Supreme Court of India has taken necessary steps by laying down the detailed provisions and guidelines for prevention and redressing of such grievances. Further, with the establishment of National Commission for Women, such issues relating with the violence against women and gender inequality are addressed and resolved in a better way. The Indian Parliament has also passed "The Sexual Harassment of

Women at Workplace (Prevention, Prohibition and Redressal) Act, 2013" which came into force from 9 December 2013. This Act seeks to protect women from sexual harassment at their work place and provides an effective grievance redressal mechanism.

The problem of female foeticide and girl infanticide is still prevalent in both the rural and urban areas of India. According to the United Nations, it is estimated that as many as 2000 girls are illegally aborted every single day and approximately as many as 15 million girls were not born in the last decade.[24] Though gender selection and abortion techniques were banned in India from 1994 under the Pre Conception and Pre Natal Diagnostics Technique Act, the use of ultrasound scanning continues even today. If this malignant practise of female foeticide and infanticide continues, then, the population of females will decline further and it will skew the sex ratio of India. It will lead to various socio-economic problems like lower female participation in employment and inefficient allocation of labour due to gender injustice. Apart from this, if this situation persists then there wouldn't be sufficient brides for marriage and it will eventually lead to a situation of marriage squeeze. That's what exactly happening in the state of Haryana where due to shortage of women for marriage, people usually marrying outside their native state and bringing brides from the other states and parts of India. Crimes like child marriages and trafficking of women have also increased over the time and led to further deterioration of the status and dignity of women.

Conclusion

To conclude, it can be said that the status of human rights and gender equality has been changing and improving around the world. In India, institutions like the Ministry for Women and Child Development, National Commission for Women and the National Human Rights Commission (constituted on 12th October 1993 under the protection of Human Rights Ordinance and was given the statutory basis), are playing a key role in protecting the rights relating to liberty, equality, and dignity of the individual guaranteed by the Constitution or embodied in the International Covenants and providing gender equality. The position of women in India is also changing with the time. From equal status with men in ancient times, through the low points during the medieval period and to the promotion and encouragement to gender equality by many reformers in the modern era, the condition of women is improving. Women are playing significant roles in the arena of politics, sports, education, arts, entertainment, literature and many more.

In global terms, the United Nations Millennium Development Goals - 3rd Goal in particular, is directly related to the empowerment of women and gender equality and it is working firmly towards achieving its goals by 2015. To honour the United Nations Universal Declaration of Human Rights, Human Rights Day is also celebrated annually across the world on December 10. India is a country which is still recovering from the years of exploitation and oppression inflicted upon the poor human beings and women in particular. As long as the mind set of the people and societal attitude will not change, talks of women's empowerment and human rights will be in vain. And this change cannot happen in an instant. It will take its time. We have still a long way to go but hopefully we will reach there someday.

References

1.   Sepulveda et al. 2004, p. 3 (1)

2.   http://usatoday30.usatoday.com/news/ topstories /2011-01-30-2052877353_x.htm

3.   Brownlie, Ian. 2003. Principles of Public International Law (6th Edition). Oxford University Press, Page – 532

4.   Universal Declaration of Human Rights, UN General Assembly, December 10, 1948. Article 217 (3)

5.   Glendon, Mary Ann, April 2004. "The Rule of Law in the Universal Declaration of Human Rights", Northwestern University Journal of International Human Rights, Volume 2:5

6.   Statute of the International Court of Justice, Chapter – 2, Competence of the Court, Article 38

7.   Yoram Dinstein, 2004. *The Conduct of Hostilities under the Law of International Armed Conflict,* pp. 5. Cambridge: Cambridge University Press

8.   Stewart, James (30 June, 2003). "Towards a Single Definition of Armed Conflict in International Humanitarian Law", International Review of the Red Cross 850: 313-350

9.   David P. Forsythe (June 17, 2007). The Internaitonal Committee of the Red Cross: A Neutral Humanitarian Actor. Routledge. Page – 43

10. Christopher Greenwood in: Fleck, Dieter, edition. 2008. The Handbook of Humanitarian Law in Armed Conflicts, Oxford University Press, pp – 27-28

11. http://www.gsdrc.org/go/topic-guides/ilfha

12. http://www.un.org/apps/news/infocusRel.asp?infocusID=114&Body=human%20rights%20council&Body1=

13. The UN Security Council referred the human rights situation in Darfur in Sudan to the International Criminal Court despite the fact that Sudan has a functioning legal system.

14. Durham, H. 2004. "We the People: The Position of NGOs in Gathering Evidence and Giving Witness in International Criminal Trials". In Thakur, R, Malcontent, P, *From Sovereign Impunity to International Accountability*, New York, United Nations University Press.

15. http://www.amnesty.org/en/death-penalty

16. Laura, Brace. 2004. The Politics of Property, Labour, Freedom and Belonging, Edinburgh University Press, pp. 162

   https://www.globalslaveryindex.org/category/press-release/-dated

17. December 27, 2013.

18. "Experts encourage action against sex trafficking", Voice of America News, May 15, 2009

19. http://web.archive.org/web/20080708202906/https:

//thereport.amnesty.org/eng/report-08-at-a-glance

20. Sutherland, Ben (March 17, 2003), "Water Forum No Talking Shop", BBC News Network

21. http://www.endpoverty2015.org/goals/gender-equity

22. Jean Dreze and Amartya Sen. 1995. India: Economic Development and Social Opportunity, Oxford University Press

23. According to a study conducted by Thomson Reuters, up to 12 million girls were aborted in India over the last 30 years

24. http://www.theguardian.com/global-development /poverty-matters/2011/may/25/india-census-alarming- sex-ratio-female-foeticide

CHAPTER
11

HUMAN RIGHTS IN THE EPOCH OF GLOBALIZATION

Jagdish Meghwal
Assistant Professor
Department of English
S.D.M. P.G. Girl's College,
Bhilwara.
(Rajasthan)

Introduction

Human rights in The Epoch Globalization are two forms of universalism, two global phenomena which, in their continuous transformation, involve in different manners the world's states.

Globalization produces opportunities and initiates changes that affect the juridical order which the International Human Rights Law is part of. This process is possible in a world where the political, cultural, economic and social relations cannot be limited by the national borders or by the state actors' will.

Technological development, communications, new

international economic and commercial agreements increase the role of international organizations and of transnational corporations, the changes at the level of international relations affect people, communities and states.

The passage to globalization acts on the economic, political rights and which are the visible consequences of this process and, at the same time, which is the role of human rights in the context of globalization are some of the questions which we intend to meditate on in these pages.

The term "globalization" was introduced by the Organization for Economic Co-operation and Development (OECD) in 1985 with reference to the process of integration of the global market by means of new economic and financial policies. The collapse of communism, the end of the Cold War, the transnational companies, the technological and informational progress opened a new stage for global communication. The definitions of globalization are multiple and contradictory. We are dealing with a political, social, but above all, an economic process1.

Economic globalization, as "market" for the actors to trade in goods and services, has lead to the creation of institutions of global nature affecting the sovereignty of the states in that they lose control of some instruments (financial, monetary, etc.) . Of course, the exchange of products has existed for centuries, but our days, it is accelerated by the development of transportation, technology, communication, computerization. The states are no longer the main and unique actors of globalization, being surpassed by the number of transnational corporations and intergovernmental institutions.

The new and old global institutions acquire an increasingly important role at global level: the World Trade Organization, the international NGOs, G7, IMF (International Monetary Fund) IBRD (The International Bank of Reconstruction and Development) but also Microsoft, CNN, EU, the Nobel Prize etc. At the same time, globalization means creating a global civil society interested in the values and norms of humanity, in justice, in human rights protection.

Globalization universalizes, this meaning the unification of societies but, at the same time of national or community identity. On the other hand, globalization particularizes, by promoting individualism and pluralism.

In turn, human rights have exceeded the national jurisdictions of states and have become part of international law, having a universal character. The global international mechanisms (the Human Rights Council, the Human Rights Committee, the Committee Against Torture etc.) or the regional ones (the European Court of Human Rights, The Inter-American Court etc.), jurisdictional or non-jurisdictional, opened the individuals' the way to the international arena as main actors, meant overcoming the state borders and authority in the fight against the violations of their rights.

 Human rights are part of the globalization process but they are also distinct from it3.The progress in communication has brought new perspectives to the world, has united people in aspirations and has made people gather in solidarity against injustice. However, there are some disadvantages in addition to such benefits, which are visible at the level of the environment, of the living standards, at the level of family as an institution of stability, threatened by the new models or even with extinction, of the private life no longer coping with the interferences, of the life within the community etc.

Law is globalized and, at the same time, human rights are too. We are noticing an increasingly alive dialogue between the juridical systems (the Romano-Germanic and the Common-law), between different legal orders (that of the Community law and the national law or that of the International Law of the classic type).

In Europe, the Court of Justice of the European Union and the European Court of Human Rights are examples of collaboration between the human rights and the market. These international jurisdictions, which, so far, have not been organically related, after having initially ignored each other, have begun to refer to each other's case-law, which obviously benefits the development of the European law. As known, the Treaty of Lisbon recorded the challenge formulated a few years ago concerned with the EU accession the European Convention on Human Rights.

We are talking about a process already under way, which will mean a new phase in the history of human rights. A certain form of globalization can be seen at the level of the international criminal courts, required to meet the need of punishing the authors of the most serious international crimes (against humanity, against peace or war crimes), where different people, opinions, legal systems and cultures have merged . Ad- hoc international criminal tribunals (for prosecuting crimes in the former Yugoslavia and Rwanda), created on the basis of some resolutions of the U.N. Security

Council, the International Criminal Court, which appeared in a conventional way, are examples of the force of the juridical acculturation process, but also of the phenomenon of globalization in this area. Internationalized courts or "hybrid jurisdictions" (such as those in Sierra Leone, Kosovo, Cambodia, Lebanon) are, in turn, vehicles of this phenomenon: the boundaries between national and international levels are exceeded, the rules and principles of the Romano-Germanic system meet those of the Common-law system, the national judges with the international ones etc. Moreover, justice becomes a means to pacify the international community, to create some spaces of dialogue.

The impact of science on human rights and the need to cover large areas of non-law or to find logical arguments and solutions determines the states to practice a permanent connection to other legislations, to stay informed, to abandon the isolation imposed by the strict respect for state sovereignty6, invites us to reflect on the concept of globalized judiciary system or on the validity of the concept of juridical order (given the dilution of the role of the national legislator and the reinforcement of the relationship between legal systems).

The distinction between national and international becomes increasingly difficult and the globalization of law acts on the juridical systems as a true fertilizer. Let's take a look, for instance, only at the effervescence produced by the Human Rights Act (1998) which makes the provisions of the European Convention on Human Rights directly applicable in the United Kingdom of Great Britain, which imposes re-reading and reinterpretation of the common-law precedents in the light of the case-law of Strasbourg7.

The impact of globalization on some categories of human laws

Globalization affects differently the internationally recognized human rights: civil, political, economic, social, cultural, the solidarity rights.

The economic rights are those that must grant a person a certain standard of living and access to development (as a right having an individual and a collective dimension). Although, logically, any economic growth (which presupposes the access to food, health, and housing by high employment and adequate salaries) should be followed by a greater protection of the economic rights, the reality is different. The investments in some countries (e.g. the African countries) come from globalized institutions (IMF, IBRD) or transnational companies and are directed to specific projects (the construction of highways, commercial companies etc.) neglecting aspects concerned with the education or the health of the population. On the other hand, the investors seek to obtain quick profits to their own interest and not to the interest of the states involved, and usually the most affected by the decisions and the priorities of the governments are the members of the poorest communities in the country. In addition, the fact that the globalized institutions use their own expertise to persuade the national governments and the involvement of the national factor is minimal, directly affects both the state sovereignty and the human rights. Finally, it should be added the risk of increasing the social inequalities by protecting the interests of the urban elites in some countries, while leaving the poor sections of the population exposed to economic exploitation.

Cultural Rights and global communication. The almost instantaneous transmission of information via satellite, the Internet communication transcends the national borders. The information on human rights is thus disseminated throughout the whole world, passing also over the political systems of the states, impeding the governments' tendencies to present in a different light the possible violations of the rights they are charged with. Information allows immediate action of NGOs or even the intervention of other states to protect the rights.

Political Rights Democracy and development are in an evident interaction. Democracy is the foundation of good governance, which is a measure of development. People's participation in political decision-making has direct implications on the quality of their lives and is part of the right to development. In the ratio between economic growth and democracy, positive and negative aspects can be identified.

Typically, the globalized institutions and the transnational companies require the partner states to meet a minimal set of conditions which are reflected at the level of respecting the democratic rules and of the transparency of the governments' or the local authorities' actions. The positive consequence may be that of determining some changes in order to attract some investments. Though, on the other hand, the perception of the political power and of the national identity is affected and the imposed conditions can lead to the distortion of the internal resources or programs.

The biggest problem is the neglect of issues concerning human rights, or that of preservation of some cultural elements within the communities. Most globalized institutions do not have in their statutes and regulations provisions to that effect. As a result, any violations of the rights of persons that a transnational company, corporation, institution etc. is charged with, will be harder to remedy via existing mechanisms which are based on the individual-state (or agent of the state) relationship. It is the states' obligation to ensure, through legislative measures, the protection of the people under their jurisdiction, regardless of the author's nature. The few exceptions are notable: the founding treaty of the European Bank for Reconstruction and Development stresses the need for development based on the democratic values. Following the criticisms of the pressure groups, recently, some conditions concerning human rights or environmental protection have also been included among the conditions imposed by the large institutions or companies. At the same time, on all possible channels, the companies and institutions are required to include at all decision-making levels and in the international treaties (such as the Multilateral Agreement on Investment and the Marrakesh Agreement Establishing the World Trade Organization) express clauses regarding human rights protection.

Perhaps the most relevant link between globalization and the political rights is represented by the European citizenship. It reunites the particular and the universal to the benefit of the human being (in all the 27 EU Member States) who may present him/herself in light of all his/her identity circles.

The European construction determines the rethinking of the concepts of citizenship and of nation-state. The creation of the single market, the free movement of persons, capitals, goods, services, and the single currency, the exchange of information, the legislative harmonization or standardization represent true challenges for the countries. Citizenship develops a sense of responsibility that exceeds the internal dimension. Compared to the classical concept, which emphasize the antagonism between the insiders and the outsiders or between "us" and "foreigners", by identifying and marginalizing the latter, the new concept is not based on contesting the other. Moreover, the trend is one of expansion, of strengthening of the term "global citizenship". The workers from the EU states or other categories of immigrants live together with the citizens of any state enjoy equal treatment in the health, education and employment systems that are they have a common status.

The economic and financial globalization determines the globalization of the life forms, of the mentalities of the individuals11. On the other hand, the single market and the Scheme system have blurred the states' borders, have spiritualized the borders in the sense of the idea formulated by N. Titulescu as early as 193212. We can talk about a "deterritorialization" of the states with a direct action on the sovereignty, which appears in new formulations13.

Citizenship has become the fundamental status of the nationals of the EU Member States. The initial idea that the "economically uninvolved" citizens are not under direct applicability of the provisions concerned with the establishment of the residence on the territory of the Member States, receives the response of the European Court of Justice14 which has decided that this right is generally applicable, and it may be limited only by the secondary legislation and through the force of the principle of proportionality. This came after the Court had previously stated that the freedom to work is important not only for creating the common market, but also as a human right to have a certain level of living.

A number of rights are granted to the citizens by the Treaty on the Functioning of the European Union: the right to access to the European institutions' documents, the right not to be discriminated against on grounds of nationality, the right to free movement and residence and work throughout the Union, the right to vote, the right to stand in local and European elections in any Member State under the same conditions as the nationals, the right to petition the European Parliament and the Ombudsman, the right to diplomatic and consular protection, the right to address the European institutions in one of the official languages of the Union.

The involvement, the activism, the responsibilities of the global citizens intend to create a global solidarity, a "spirit" of the global citizenship, to initiate and support reforms, to Create a global business elite, to found some structures independent of the states and a new political community.

Instead of Conclusions

Do human rights have to adapt to globalization? Or is it necessary to reinforce the international systems of protection? The international mechanism, as pointed out, was set in motion. The fact that the generalization of the clauses for the protection of the rights is imposed in the economic agreements and contracts represents an important step. On the other hand, bringing multinational corporations before international or state jurisdictions for human rights violations is a sign of reinforcement. There remain open the paths to bring human rights up to date and also those of international cooperation which goes beyond the vision of a globalizead law only s a response to the aspects of the market economy, the competition, and which ensures strong connections between the economic, social, criminal etc. aspects.

References

1. Alex,Y. Seita. 1997. Globalization and the Convergence of Values, 30 Cornell International Law. pp. 429.

2. Richard, Falk. The Making of Global Citizenship, in Global Visions: Beyond the NewIbidem.

3. Patrick, Artus, Marie-Paule, Virard. 2005. Globalisation, Le pire est à venir, La Découverte, Paris. pp.13.

4. Julie, Allard., Antoine, Garapon. 2005. Les juges dans la mondialisation. nouvelle révolution du droit, Édition du Seuil et La Republique des Idées, pp.30.

5. Pascal, Bruckner. 2006. The Tyranny of Penitence, Trei Publishing House. pp. 164.

6. Richard, Falk.1993.The Making of Global Citizenship, in Global Visions: Beyond the New World Order, 1993 Jeremy Breche Eds.,

7. Julie Allard, Antoine Garapon, Les juges dans la mondialisation. La nouvelle révolution du droit, Édition du Seuil etLa République des Idées, 2005

8. Patrick Artus, Marie - Paule Virard, Globalisation, Lepireestàvenir, La Découverte, Paris, 2005

9. See Michael Byers, The Meaning of Global Citizenship,

2005.

10. Jorn. Rűsen, Hans-Klaus Keul, Adrian-Paul Iliescu, Human Rights at the Meeting ofCultures, Paralela 45 Publishing House, 2004, p.159.

11. N. Titulescu. 1967. Diplomatic Documents, Politic Publishing House, Bucharest. pp. 400.

12. Bogdan, Aurescu,. 2003. The New Sovereignty, ALL Beck Publishing House, pp. 114.

13. Case C-413/99, Baumbast and R vs. Secretary of Statefor the Home Department, para.85-91.

CHAPTER
12

HUMAN RIGHTS AND ENVIRONMENT: ACHIEVEMENTS, CHALLENGES & PERSPECTIVES

Chandra Gurnani, Shinam Mukhija, Abha Dhingra
Department of Biosciences
D.V.A. College
Sri Ganganagar
(Rajasthan)

Vikram Kumar
Department of Biology
GSSS Talwara Khurd,
Ellanabad, Sirsa
(Haryana)

Introduction

If we look at society from a historical perspective, we realize that protection and preservation of the environment has been integral to the cultural and religious ethos of most human communities. Nature has been venerated by ancient Hindus, Greeks, Native Americans and other religions around the world. They worshipped all forms of nature believing that it emanated the spirit of God. Hinduism declared in its dictum that "the Earth is our mother and we are all her children." (Atharva Veda). The ancient Greeks worshipped Gaea or the Earth Goddess. Islamic law regards man as having inherited "all the resources of life and nature" and having certain religious duties to God in using those (Islamic Principles 1983). In the Judeo-Christian tradition, God gave the earth to his people and their offspring as an everlasting possession, to be cared for and passed on to each generation (Genesis).

Man is the best creativity of the God. In turn he sums up his experiences and others also and go on discovering, inventing, creating and advancing. Man has the ability of transforming his surroundings. While doing so he can develop and enhance the quality of life for his fellow human beings. But, when heedlessly applied the same creativity can cause harm to the environment. Thus, since the beginning of the earth he benefited the earth and with same zeal caused harm also. One can observe this destruction in every field. He polluted the water; he polluted the air, caused harm to the living beings on earth, land and in the sky. Because of his actions the ecological balance is disturbed. The actions of man caused harm to the physical, social and mental health of his fellow human beings. Natural resources are drained. Ozone layer is depleted.

Problems

The main problem for all the evils is the population blast. Though the population rate all over the world got reduced- the population still continues to grow. While taking measures for the preservation of the environment while framing the policies in this direction this fact should be borne in mind. This does not mean we ignore people. Of all things in the world, people are the most precious. But, they are the reason behind environmental degradation. Along with the population, natural resources should increase. There should be a good balance between the population growth and environmental protection. So this led to formulation of environmental laws.

> ➤ Early examples of legal enactments designed to consciously preserve the environment, for its own sake or human enjoyment, are found throughout history. In the common law, the primary protection was found in the law of nuisance, but this only allowed for private actions for damages or injunctions if there was harm to land. Thus smells emanating from pig stys(Aldred's Case 1610), strict liability against dumping rubbish (R v Stephens 1866) or damage from exploding dams (Rylands v Fletcher 1868). Private enforcement, however, was limited and found to be woefully inadequate to deal with major environmental threats, particularly threats to common resources. During the "Great Stink" of 1858, the dumping of sewerage into the River Thames began to smell so ghastly in the summer heat that Parliament had to be evacuated. Ironically, the Metropolitan Commission of Sewers Act 1848 had allowed the Metropolitan Commission for Sewers to close cesspits around the city in an attempt to "clean up" but this simply led people to pollute the river. In 19 days, Parliament passed a further Act to build the

London sewerage system. London also suffered from terrible air pollution, and this culminated in the "Great Smog" of 1952, which in turn triggered it's on legislative response: the Clean Air Act 1956. The basic regulatory structure was to set limits on emissions for households and business (particularly burning coal) while an inspectorate would enforce compliance. Environmental issues received attention after 43 years in Stockholm conference, 1972. Many programs were started to protect environment.

➢ Celebration of "World Environment Day" 5th June initiated.

➢ Many other Environmental Conferences:

▪ United Nations Conference on Environment and development, Rio de Janerio in 1992- "Earth Summit"

▪ World Summit on Sustainable Development, Johannesburg in 2002

▪ Copenhagen Conference, 2007

➢ Award of Nobel Peace prize to environmentalists in 2004 and 2007

➢ Indian Culture is based on Principles of environmental Conservation. Since prehistoric times Indians protected the Mother Nature.The concept of keeping forest reserves was first developed by Kautilya, an Indian scholar in the past.

➢ Trees of different species are protected and preserved

as sacred grovesin most parts of the country. Our Vedas are enriched with values of Sun, Water, Mountains, Riversand Animals. There is an unparalleled example of "Chipko Movement" in 1973 for Khejri tree.

➢ Van- Panchayats in U.P.

Environmental Laws

In India, Environmental law is governed by the Environment Protection Act, 1986. This act is enforced by the Central Pollution Control Board and the numerous State Pollution Control Boards. Apart from this, there are also individual legislations specifically enacted for the protection of Water, Air, Wildlife, etc.

Although environmental protection and human rights are often treated as separate legal topics, there are many situations where the two fields intersect, for example, with respect to the rights of indigenous people. First, many governments and international bodies have recognized the right of citizens to live in a clean and healthful environment. Second, environmental and natural resources policies may disproportionately affect poor and minority communities. For instance, in the United States the placing of local government landfills in primarily Latino and African-American neighbourhoods may constitute a violation of the Equal Protection Clause (under the 14th Amendment to the U.S. Constitution).

The situation of human rights in India is a complex one, as a result of the country's large size and tremendous diversity, its status as a developing country and a sovereign, secular, democratic, republic. The constitution of India provides for Fundamental rights, which include freedom of religion. Human rights and environmental law have traditionally been envisaged as two distinct, independent spheres of rights. Towards the last quarter of the 20th century, however, the perception arose that the cause of protection of the environment could be promoted by setting it in the framework of human rights, which had by then been firmly established as a matter of international law and practice.

In light of the breadth of environmental law and policy, and the manner in which it intrudes into every aspect of environmental protection in an international sense and notwithstanding the concept of state sovereignty, it is argued that it is unnecessary to have a separate human right to a decent environment.This view militates against the confusion of the two distinct spheres of human rights law and environmental law. However, there are many who oppose this view.

Human Health and Human Rights

At present, human health is the bridge between human rights and environmental protection, being a primary objective of both areas of regulation. Human rights exist to promote and protect human well-being, to allow the full development of each person and the maximization of the person's goals and interests, individually and in community with others. This cannot occur without basic conditions of health, which the state is to promote and protect.

Articulating a right to a decent or healthy environment within the context of economic, social, and cultural rights is not inherently problematic. Clarifying the existence of such a right would entail giving greater weight to the global public interest in protecting the environment and promoting sustainable development, but this could be achieved without doing damage to the fabric of human rights law, and in a manner which fully respects the wide margin of appreciation that states are entitled to exercise when balancing economic, environmental, and social policy objectives. It would build on existing precedents under the ICESCR, and reflect international policy on sustainable development endorsed at Rio in 1992 and in subsequent international conferences. The further elaboration of procedural rights, based on the Aarhus Convention, would facilitate the implementation of such a right, and give greater prominence globally to the role of NGOs in public interest litigation and advocacy. These two developments go hand in hand. They are not a necessary part of any declaration or protocol on human rights and the environment, but they do represent a logical extension of existing policies and would represent a real exercise in progressive development of the law. A declaration or protocol on human rights and the environment thus makes sense provided it brings together existing civil, political, economic, and social rights in one coherent whole, while at the same time reconceptualising in the language of economic and social rights the idea of the environment as a common good. It would, in other words, recognize the global environment as a public interest that states have a responsibility to protect, even if they only implement that responsibility progressively and insofar as resources allow.

Using existing human rights law to grapple with climate change is more challenging. Giving human rights extraterritorial scope in environmental cases is not the problematic issue, however as we have seen, the argument that transboundary victims come within the jurisdiction or control of the polluting state can be made, is consistent with existing human rights law, and is supported by developments in international environmental law. If that is correct then a state does have to take account of transboundary environmental impacts on human rights and it is obliged to facilitate access to remedies and other procedures. But climate change is a global problem. It cannot easily be addressed by the simple process of giving existing human rights law transboundary effect. Moreover, much of the economic policy which drives greenhouse gas emissions worldwide is presently lawful and consistent with the terms of the UNFCCC and the Kyoto Protocol. It is no more likely to be derailed by human rights litigation based on ICCPR rights than the UK's policy on Heathrow airport in the Hatton Case. The response of human rights law – if it is to have one - needs to be in global terms, treating the global environment and climate as the common concern of humanity. That is why locating the right to a decent environment within the corpus and institutional structures of economic, social, and cultural rights makes more sense. In that context the policies of individual states on energy use, reduction of greenhouse gas emissions, land use, and deforestation could be scrutinized and balanced against the evidence of their global impact on human rights and the environment. This is not a panacea for deadlock in the UNFCCC negotiations, but it would give the rights of humanity as a whole a voice that at present is scarcely heard. Whether the UNHRC wishes to travel down this road is another question, for politicians to answer rather than lawyers, but that is where it must go if it wishes to do more than posture on climate change.

Assessing the influence of political liberties and civil rights on the environment is not straightforward. There is little empirical evidence of a direct link, and research is hampered by a lack of national-level data on environmental conditions outside industrialized countries. It deals with how the gardeners can play an important role in environmental protection as well as in reducing the global warming.

Environmental Courts

In India there is a need of separate environmental courts. There are thousands cases pending in court. This is leading to greater loss to ecosystem of which human is also a part.

In the Judgment of the Supreme Court of India in A.P. Pollution Control Board vs. M.V. Nayudu, the Court referred to the need for establishing Environmental Courts which would have the benefit of expert advice from environmental scientists/technically qualified persons, as part of the judicial process, after an elaborate discussion of the views of jurists in various countries. In the subsequent follow-up judgment in A.P. Pollution Control Board vs. M.V. Nayudu, the Supreme Court, referred to the serious differences in the constitution of appellate authorities under plenary as well as delegated legislation and pointed out that except in one State where the appellate authority was manned by a retired High Court

Judge, in other States they were manned only by bureaucrats. These appellate authorities were not having either judicial or environment back-up on the Bench. The needs for Environmental Courts were advocated in two earlier judgments also. One was M.C. Mehta v. Union of India where the Supreme Court said that in as much as environment cases involve assessment of scientific data; it was desirable to set up environment courts on a regional basis with a professional Judge and two experts, keeping in view the expertise required for such adjudication. There should be an appeal Court observed that Environmental Courts having civil and criminal jurisdiction must be established to deal with the environmental issues in a speedy manner. It is important to note here that the National Environmental Appellate Authority constituted under the National Environmental Appellate Authority Act, 1997, for the limited purpose of providing a forum to review the administrative decisions on Environment Impact Assessment, had very little work. It has to be noted that since the year 2000, no Judicial Member has been appointed. So far as the National Environmental Tribunal Act, 1995 is concerned, the legislation has yet to be notified despite the expiry of eight years.

Since it was enacted by Parliament, the Tribunal under the Act is yet to be constituted. Thus, these two Tribunals are non-functional and remain only on paper. In view of the observations of the Supreme Court in the above said judgments, and having regard to the inadequacies of the existing appellate authorities, - which neither contain judges nor have the assistance of experts - and their limited jurisdiction, - this Project proposes to review the position with a view to bring uniformity in the constitution of these bodies and the scope of their jurisdiction. There arises a need to constitute specialized 'environment courts' and should consist of judicial members assisted by technical experts. The court should be located along with all the other High Courts with a higher Appellate Authority. The Environment Court should exercise original as well as appellate jurisdiction. It should be able to grant all orders which a Civil Court could grant, including the grant of 'compensation' as visualized by the National Environmental Tribunal Act, 1995. Access to justice, particularly, in matters relating to environment, is an essential facet of Article 21 of the Constitution of India. We can conclude with a set of concepts of Human Right and Environmental Protection and their provisions under Indian and international laws and after finding the linkage between both and their prevailing condition in India and a thorough study of Judicial activism i.e. the role of judiciary on Environmental Protection and Human Rights, that there is a close connection between the protection of human rights and environmental protection in the context of sustainable development. They reflect the growing interrelationship between approaches to ensuring human rights and environmental protection.

Suggestions

In this reference, our suggestion is that to protect the human rights as well as environment. It is essential for the protection of Environment to create the awareness in the society and government should establish Environmental Tribunal for speedy trial and justice and consciousness of the society. The quantum of punishment (Civil & Criminal) under the Environmental Laws should be enhanced according to gravity of the damages to environment and public.

References

1. Atharva Veda (Bhumi Sukta).

2. Islamic Principles for the Conservation of the Natural Environment, 13-14 (IUCN and Saudi Arabia, 1983).

3. Genesis1:1-31, 17:7-8.

4. Aldred's Case (1610) 9 Co Rep 57b; 77 ER 816

5. R V Stephens (1866) LR 1 QB 702.

6. Rylands V Fletcher (1868) UKHL 1.

7. The Environment Protection Act 1986. envfor.nic.in. Retrieved 2015-08-27.

CHAPTER
13

LINKAGE BETWEEN HUMAN RIGHTS AND ENVIRONMENT

Dr. Shyam S. Khinchi
Associate Professor & Head
Department of Geography
Dr. Bhim Rao Ambedkar Govt. P.G. College,
Sri Ganganagar
(Rajasthan)

Dr. Deepak Kamble
Associate Professor & Head
Department of Geography
DKASC College,
Lchalkaranji, Kohlapur
(Maharastra)

Introduction

Consistently, more than 2 million died and billions of instances of sicknesses are credited to contamination. Individuals encounter the negative impacts of ecological debasement everywhere throughout the world. These corruptions incorporate water deficiency, fisheries exhaustion, characteristic catastrophes because of deforestation and hazardous administration and transfer of harmful and perilous squanders and items. The environmental change is worsening a large portion of these negative impacts of ecological corruption on human wellbeing and the prosperity and is additionally bringing about new ones, for example, the expansion in outrageous climate occasions. Along these lines these realities obviously demonstrate the nearby linkages between the earth and the satisfaction in human rights. This is additionally the motivation behind why a coordinated way to deal with environment and human rights is defended. In 2009, the UN Environment Program and the Office of the High Commissioner for Human Rights talked about the arrangement of resolutions embraced by the UN Human Rights Council on the relationship between a sheltered and solid environment and the happiness regarding human rights. The point of the UNEP is to illuminate and increment consciousness of the linkage between human rights and natural law, and at last to move towards acknowledgment of a crucial human ideal to a sound domain. In this exposition the immediate and circuitous connections between the assurance of nature and the pleasure in human rights will be drawn.

Legal Aspects

There exist three principle measurements of the interrelationship between human rights and ecological assurance:

1. The earth as an essential for the happiness regarding

human rights.

2.　Certain human rights, particularly the entrance to data, interest of the general population in basic leadership, and the entrance to equity in ecological matters, as basic to great natural basic leadership and

3.　The rights to a protected, solid and environmentally adjusted environment as a human ideal in itself.

In 1972, the Stockholm Declaration on the Human Environment broadcasted, that: "Man has the major ideal to flexibility, fairness and satisfactory states of life, in a situation of a quality that allows an existence of pride and prosperity." After this announcement, an enduring level headed discussion concerning details of the privilege to a sound domain had begun. An immeasurable number of inquiries have encircled this exchange, for example, What is the advantage of planning another privilege to a solid domain? What is the substance of the privilege? Does universal law perceive a privilege to a solid situation?

Following four many years of dialogs concerning the linkages between human rights and the earth, a few key advancements have added to the worldwide community`s comprehension of these linkages. A noteworthy number of worldwide instruments, including arrangements, universal resolutions and statements, have explained certain parts of the human rights and nature association. Additionally the it's proclaimed that Environment and Development accentuates the need to incorporate environment and advancement keeping in mind the end goal to accomplish maintainable improvement and take into account a solid and gainful life in congruity alongside nature. Facilitate on, a high number of multilateral natural assentation's perceive the connection between the earth and human wellbeing. These MEAs incorporate arrangements in regards to revelation of natural data and open investment in basic leadership. Essentially, local human rights bargains in Africa and South America expressly allude to one side to live in a sound domain through various plans. It can be held, that the Stockholm Declaration and to a specific degree likewise, indicate how the connection between human rights and nature has as of now been very noticeable in the early phases of United Nations endeavors to address the ecological issues, despite the fact that the human rights angle is not expressly made in the greater part of these instruments.

Likewise, uncommon techniques built up under the UN human rights framework have added to elucidating certain measurements of the human rights and the earth linkages, for example, regarding dangerous waste, indigenous people groups rights, nourishment, water and environmental change. Moreover, in March 2012, the UN Human Rights Council made a three-year command for an "Autonomous Expert on Human Rights and the Environment." This free master is asked for, to concentrate the human rights commitments in regards to one side to a sheltered, spotless, solid and practical environment and to present a report, including conclusions and proposals, to the Council.

Evaluation of Environment and Human Right Link

Hearing and having to decide on human rights and environment cases has forced regional and universal supervisory mechanisms to address the human rights and the environment linkage. There are examples of human rights mechanisms, that have addressed the right to a healthy environment directly, and other examples where they have addressed the environmental dimensions of the right to life, the right to property, the right to private life, and the right to access to information, which are rights directly implicated in human rights and the environment case law. The jurisprudence which resulted, represents an important contribution to the international community`s understanding of the human rights and the environment linkage.

So therefore, it is possible to state that environmental law has evolved to not only incorporate but also influence human rights law. Environmental instruments increasingly include human rights protections and principles, including specific procedural rights. Environmental law has also evolved to recognize substantive rights with relation to the environment, such as the rights to be free from toxic pollutions. At the same time, developing environmental norms have influenced human rights law. This can be described as the greening of human rights law. The greening is evident in decisions of international tribunals, which progressively take into account environmental threats, which undermine human rights.

Rights of Protection

The preservation and assurance of the earth is connected to both, procedural and substantive rights. It is additionally connected to political and social liberties, and additionally social, monetary and social rights, constructive and pessimistic rights, individual and aggregate rights and rights that are related with humankind overall – and particularly rights that are held by the living individuals and even rights held by future eras. This part of the exposition will talk about the principle substantive and procedural human rights that are connected to nature in global law.

a) Functional Law

In universal law, the natural parts of various substantive human rights have been tended to. These incorporate, among others, common and political rights, for example, the rights to life, religion and property; and social and social rights, for example, the privilege to wellbeing, water and nourishment. Every so often, human rights systems have tended to one side to a solid domain straightforwardly. Be that as it may, chiefly they have tended to the natural parts of more settled rights; albeit developing rights, for example, the privilege to water, have assumed real parts. Yet, natural administrations have likewise addressed individual rights, by giving risk and pay instruments. These components suggest acknowledgment of lawfully cognizable interests in property and wellbeing. Additionally, both human rights and natural law perceive aggregate rights embroiled by ecological corruption, for instance rights held by indigenous individuals. At last, ecological instruments and global tribunals have specified rights held by future eras.

Promote more, the impacts of ecological debasement on human welfare have been perceived by human rights and by natural law. There are a considerable measure of MEAs that perceive the connection between the earth and human wellbeing and prosperity. A considerable lot of the MEAs additionally incorporate arrangements with respect to common obligation and pay for harm brought on by ecological corruption, especially with regards to contamination and human rights tribunals have discovered infringement of perceived privileges of life, property, wellbeing and a solid domain created by natural variables.

b) Procedural Law

Rights to access to data, cooperation in basic leadership, and access to equity are found in both human rights and natural instruments, and have been deciphered under both administrations to give wide securities to ecological interests. This makes procedural rights a key purpose of convergence amongst ecological and human rights law. For the insurance of the indigenous habitat, the assurance and advancement of procedural rights has been, and keeps on being significant. Guideline 10 of the proclaims, "Ecological issues are best taken care of with interest of every concerned national, at the pertinent level." This rule had a critical effect on the accentuation on procedural rights in a natural setting. Not exclusively does it express that people ought to have fitting access to data, additionally that people ought to be able to take an interest in basic leadership forms and that they ought to have admittance to legal and managerial procedures, including review and cure.

Another essential understanding is the Aarhus Convention. In spite of the fact that working primarily at a provincial level, it has turned into the most noteworthy universal natural assertion ensuring procedural human rights. The convention`s introduction announces the privilege of everybody to live in a situation satisfactory to his or her wellbeing and prosperity. Article 1 assist on accommodates privileges of access to data, open support and access to equity. Other than the Aarhus Convention, various consequent MEAs embraced in the 1990s likewise joined least measures for access to data and investment. Procedural rights, including privileges of data, cooperation, and access to equity, have been perceived with regards to provincial and worldwide human rights instruments too. The European Court of Justice, for instance, has found that "long regulatory procedures to seek after a natural right may disregard the Article 6 appropriate to reasonable hearing inside a sensible time.

Implementation

In the field of global human rights and universal environment, the execution and requirement endeavors confront significant difficulties. Be that as it may, likewise in national level, there is an absence of will for usage. Russia is a flawless case for a nation, which has a standout amongst the most explained natural enactment on the planet, while in the meantime just a little number of that enactment has been executed up until this point, because of absence of political will.

There is still an extensive crevice between general human rights arrangements and their usage – and that hole obviously remains when the human rights and the earth linkage becomes possibly the most important factor. By the by, there are an assortment of instruments accessible. Aside from the worldwide and territorial courts and tribunals, consideration ought to likewise be attracted towards to the International Criminal Court, the World Trade Organizations, the World Bank and MEA Secretariats. Notwithstanding the worldwide instruments deduced in the most recent 40 years that fortify the human rights and the earth linkage, the statute of widespread and territorial human rights supervisory systems has handled the natural measurement of ensured human rights. The case law of local human rights courts reacts to applications by casualties and common society associations, looking for reparation for human rights encroachments brought about by ecological contamination. Hearing and choosing human rights and the earth cases has constrained provincial and general supervisory instruments to address the human rights and nature linkage to an ever increasing extent.

Mechanisms

In the field of global human rights and universal environment, the execution and requirement endeavors confront significant difficulties. Be that as it may, likewise in national level, there is an absence of will for usage. Russia is a flawless case for a nation, which has a standout amongst the most explained natural enactment on the planet, while in the meantime just a little number of that enactment has been executed up until this point, because of absence of political will. There is still an extensive crevice between general human rights arrangements and their usage and that hole obviously remains when the human rights and the earth linkage becomes possibly the most important factor. By the by, there are an assortment of instruments accessible. Aside from the worldwide and territorial courts and tribunals, consideration ought to likewise be attracted towards to the International Criminal Court, the World Trade Organizations, the World Bank and MEA Secretariats.

Notwithstanding the worldwide instruments deduced in the

most recent 40 years that fortify the human rights and the earth linkage, the statute of widespread and territorial human rights supervisory systems has handled the natural measurement of ensured human rights. The case law of local human rights courts reacts to applications by casualties and common society associations, looking for reparation for human rights encroachments brought about by ecological contamination. Hearing and choosing human rights and the earth cases has constrained provincial and general supervisory instruments to address the human rights and nature linkage to an ever increasing extent.

c) Mechanism of Law of Human Right

Since the UN Conference on the Human Environment in 1972, the linkage between human rights and the earth has been reinforced globally. Human rights law has after some time perceived the basic significance of the earth.

In the later universal human rights instruments, they unequivocally perceive linkages between human rights and the earth, especially with regards to one side to sustenance, the privilege to wellbeing, and indigenous rights to property, regular assets, and culture. While more seasoned human rights arrangements drafted and embraced before ecological assurance turned into a matter of worldwide concern do exclude unequivocal references to natural issues, they do ensure interests straightforwardly influenced by ecological debasement. Human rights settlement bodies and the territorial human rights systems have more than once translated these instruments in a way that perceives the natural measurement of these ensured rights, including the rights to life, wellbeing, sustenance, and water. Human rights instruments additionally build up procedural rights applicable to ecological assurance, for example, the rights to data, equity and investment in basic leadership. These rights are vital to permitting people and gatherings to secure their ecological advantages.

d) Mechanism of Global Human Rights

United Nation: The primary lawful restricting instrument to be said is the Charter of United Nations. This Charter, has global legitimacy, went into constrained on October 1945 and sets out the reasons for the UN, including the security of human rights. Albeit natural issues are not explicitly said in the UN Charter, the social and monetary arrangements (Article 55 of the Charter) establish the framework for the elaboration of human rights to consolidate ecological security. Ecological corruption influences the way of life, wellbeing and social advance contrarily and makes natural security vital to accomplishing the Charter`s objectives. The necessity, that states advance regard for these social and monetary interests and also human rights and principal flexibility, fabricate a reason for forcing positive commitments to secure the regular habitat.

Geneva Conventions: The Protocol Additional to the Geneva Conventions identifying with the Protection of Victims of International Armed Conflicts (Protocol I), addresses ecological pulverization coming about because of worldwide equipped clashes. Article 54 II forbids activity "to assault, demolish, evacuate or render pointless items fundamental to the survival of the nonmilitary personnel populace, for example, nourishment stuffs, rural territories for the generation of sustenance stuffs, crops, domesticated animals, drinking water establishment and supplies and water systems works." Other than that, Article 55 all the more critically, accommodates the security of the indigenous habitat. It gives, that "care might be taken in fighting to secure the indigenous habitat against boundless, long haul and extreme harm" and incorporates a disallowance of the utilization of the strategies or method for fighting which are proposed or might be relied upon to bring about such harm to the regular habitat. Moreover, assaults against the common habitat by method for retaliations are disallowed.

e) Mechanism of Environmental Law

Natural instruments outline ecological insurance both inherent and instrumental. The instruments do perceive the significance of ecological issues to human wellbeing, welfare, and monetary advancement. Their worry is the relationship between ecological discussion and property rights and social rights. This acknowledgment of the named relationship gives a premise to a contention for the need of saving the earth to secure human rights and not just the other way around. In the field of worldwide law, Principle 21 of the Stockholm Declaration has risen as the standard portrayal of the linkage amongst power and global commitment. It gives that states have the sovereign ideal to abuse their own particular assets, yet in the meantime they have the duty to guarantee that all exercises inside their ward or control don't make harm the earth of different states or of ranges past the breaking points of national purview. However, truth be told, numerous natural instruments go past this, in perceiving parts of the earth as segments of the basic legacy of mankind. This idea shows up as the idea of "basic legacy of humankind" and "world legacy of humankind all in all" and is found in a few traditions, for example, the World Heritage Convention. This idea is further identified with the idea of "normal enthusiasm of humankind" that is expressed in the Outer Space Treaty and the "regular worry of mankind" which is expressed in the UN Framework Convention on Climate Change. Each of the named arrangements portrays security of the earth either as a lawfully cognizable intrigue or as concern held aggregately by the humanity all in all. This approach makes a commitment upon all states to attempt endeavors into concerning the normal legacy assets inside their own regions, notwithstanding when they don't cross national limits, with a positive result in the field of ecological law.

Conclusion

Gone up against with the aftereffects of dirtying and ruinous human activities, numerous worldwide and local bargains and neighborhood laws on environment assurance have been presented. As we have seen, these settlements did not say human rights in connection to ecological assurance at first. Be that as it may, amid the past 40 years, the connections between human rights and nature have continuously been perceived.

People rely on upon securing nature as the asset base for all life. Individuals everywhere throughout the world began to see increasingly that a perfect and solid environment is basic to the acknowledgment of major human rights, for example, the privilege to life, wellbeing and advancement. What's more, since the unimportant linkage between human rights to instances of natural interruption crystalized, throughout the years it has turned out to be significantly more recognized that human rights and the earth are so intrinsically interlinked that one can express that a perfect and solid environment is a human right. As of now, there are a few worldwide and territorial human rights sanctions and assentation's, that give unequivocal controls of a human right environment.

These methodologies have demonstrated the significance and the raising cognizance among the general population about a perfect and solid environment everywhere throughout the world. The question is currently, what ought to the following strides be, that should be taken to achieve a far reaching all inclusive ecological security?.Such a conceivable stride could be to imagine, recognize, build up and regard the universal human appropriate to a spotless and solid environment, at a national or provincial level, as well as above all at an UN level.

References

1.   Ademi, Fatlum. The Linkage Between Human Rights and Environmental, Environmental Law in an International Context, Lund University

2.   Anton, D. K. and Shelton, D. L. 2011. Environmental Protection and Human Rights, Cambridge University Press, New York, p.436.

3.   Birnie, P., Boyle, A. and Redgewell, C. 2009. International Law & the Environment, 3rd edition, Oxford University Press, New York. pp. 271

4.   Craik, N. 2008. The International Law of Environmental Impact Assessment - Process, Substance and

Integration, Cambridge University Press, New York. pp.87.

5.   Craik, N. 2008. The International Law of Environmental Impact Assessment – Process, Substance and Integration, Cambridge University Press, New York. pp. 96.

6.   Dées V. Hungary, European Court of Human Rights, App. No. 2345 / 06 (2010).

7.   ESCR Committee, General Comment No. 14: The Right to the Highest Attainable Standard of Health, 2000.

8.   Giacomelli V. Italy, European Court of Human Rights, App. No. 599009 /00 (2006).

9.   Handl, G.1995. Human Rights and Protection of the Environment: A Mildly Revisionist View, in: A. C. Trindade (ed.), Human Rights and Environmental Protection. pp.117.

10.   http://www.humanrights.ch/de/internationale-menschenrechte/nachrichten/menschenrechtsrat/umweltschutz-perspektive-menschenrechte, 2015 -05-31.

11.   http://www.unep.org/delc/HumanRightsandTheEnvironment/tabid/54409/Default.aspx, 2015-05-31

12.   Humphreys, S. 2009. Competing Claims: Human Rights and Climate Harms, in: S. Humphreys (ed.) Human Rights and Climate Change, Cambridge University Press, New York. pp. 37.

13.   Kiss, A. and Shelton, D. 2007. Guide to International Environmental Law, Martinus Nijhoff Publishers, Leiden/Boston. pp.37.

14.   Protocol on Environmental Protection to the Antarctic Treaty, October 4, 1991.

15.   Rodriguez-Rivera, L.E. 2001. Is the Human Right to Environment Recognized under International Law? It Depends on the Source, in: Colorado Journal of International and Environmental Law and Policy. pp. 41.

16.   UNECE Convention on Access to Information, Public Participation and Access to Justice in Environmental Matters (Aarhus, June 25, 1998).

17.   UNEP Compendium on Human Rights and the Environment, Nairobi, 2009, pp. 12

18.   UNEP Compendium on Human Rights and the Environment, Nairobi, 2009, pp. 14.

29.   UNEP Compendium on Human Rights and the Environment, Nairobi. 2009, pp. 7.

CHAPTER
14

REALITIES OF HUMAN RIGHTS AND TRIBAL PEOPLE LIVES IN INDIA: A STUDY

Dr. Sunil Kumar Verma
Assistant Professor
Department of Geography
Dr. B.R. Ambedkar Govt. P.G. College,
Sri Ganganagar
(Rajasthan)

Introduction

The Tribal individuals in India have a long history even before the entry of the pilgrim government. The Tribal social orders that existed preceding the pioneer intercession had their own particular rights and obligations inside their independent sovereign structure. Aside from the experience of the Tribals with the different civic establishments, there was additionally the impact of the outside ministers in the past and of the overwhelming society through the fundamentalist strengths in the current past. There is a little uncertainty that Tribal people group keep on being the most underestimated gathering in India. Social markers of advancements tell that Tribal individuals have futures that are decades shorter than the non-tribal are. Some other social pointer, be it measures of wellbeing offices training openings and accomplishment, level of business or standard of lodging, sees Tribal people group getting a charge out of less open doors, and enduring more noteworthy weights, than whatever remains of the Indian populace.

Tribal Community Rights

Human rights are the bequests of each person and they shape an essential part of the socio-social texture of humankind everywhere throughout the world. In any case, they are helpless against manhandle and infringement. Human rights can be comprehended as dynamic standards and qualities ensured in laws, constitutions, and universal traditions. In the meantime, human rights are social ideas that are gradually developing because of social change or contestation (Nair Ravi, 2006). The paper investigates how human rights have turned out to be appropriate to the substances of Tribal lives, and how we can expand on the global traditions and assentions that have fulfilled this undertaking to comprehend the measurements of Tribals' human rights in the Indian culture. Tribals' human rights give crucial bits of knowledge into the causes, appearances and results of human rights infringement experienced by Tribal people group. In India, the last quarter of the twentieth century has been an observer to the developing acknowledgment of the place and importance of human rights because of weight from different aggregate developments. Clearly this worry in human rights is established in the disavowal of life and freedom that was an unavoidable part of the crisis (1975–77). The mass captures of the pioneers of the resistance and the focused on dread of the individuals who could exhibit a test to a dictator state are a portion of the predominant pictures that have survived. The common freedoms development was a result of the emergency. Anticipating subjective confinement, detainment, the utilization of the legal procedure non-straightforwardly and custodial savagery were on the motivation of the common freedoms development. For recent decades, developments of laborers, tribals, Dalits, ladies, understudies and average workers developments have highlighted human rights concerns (Shah, 2004)

In this manner, human rights have turned out to be noticeable on the national and global plan. Harmonizing with the United Nation Declaration, the Indian Constitution likewise duplicates that, the State won't recognize against any native on grounds of birth, place, ethnic, religion, standing and concurred that the advancement and assurance of every human right is a honest to goodness worry of the State. These incorporate fundamental survival rights to human services, sanctuary, nourishment and standardized savings; the privilege to work; the privilege to instruction; and the privilege to take an interest in the social existence of one's general public. Notwithstanding, there is an enormous hole between the perfect of the human rights laws and the truth of proceeding with gross human rights infringement of Tribal people group in India.

Non-Tribal Land Disaffection

The protected defends as gave in the fifth Schedule of the Constitution of India and different other State level laws which among others restrict exchange of the grounds of the

Tribal people group have neglected to anticipate boundless land estrangement of the Tribal individuals. The center reason for the land distance has been the Land Acquisition Act-1894 under which the administration can practice its sovereign energy to take away any land for the sake of public purposes‖. The non-tribals have likewise illicitly involved hundreds sections of land of land having a place with Tribal people group by compel in Andhra Pradesh, allurement and procuring Tribal terrains by wedding Tribal ladies. There is plentiful of confirmations that a lion's share of these non-tribals is from waterfront Andhra upper rank and governing classes. Numerous researchers who chipped away at Tribal issues have raised these issues all the time. Indeed, even Girglani, J.M in his cover Tribal Land issues in Telangana Area' submitted to the Government in 2005 says that Telangana have been losing area to non-tribals since long back. The Gonds of Adilabad in the 1930s lost land to Marathis and amid 1940s to Hindu and Muslim pioneers welcomed by the Nizam from neighboring locale. The renowned Regulation of Scheduled ranges in Telangana saw an entry of non-tribal populace, which at the appointed time of time has gone under the control of Telugu non-tribals for the most part from four focal waterfront Andhra locale. The invasion of non-tribals from coastal regions over booked regions in Telangana proceeded with unabated. As per gauges as much as 1.5 lakhs sections of land of ripe grounds along Godavari River banks of Warangal and Khammam have gone into hands of prevailing position individuals, for example, Kamma, Rajulu, Reddy and Kapu landowners and cultivators having a place with the waterfront territory because of incapable execution of the Land Transfer Regulation Acts. In comparative lines with Kerala, Andhra Pradesh Land Transfer

Regulation-1959 was changed in 1970, trying to suit the enthusiasm of non-tribals therefore Khammam region has turned into a casualty to most frightful non-tribals infiltration from beach front zones.

Forest Right Non Deficiency

After the rise of private property and the development of present day country states, as Tribal people group have no legitimate rights over the grounds they have been living on and developing for eras, it turned out to be simple for the non-tribals to procure the place where there is Tribal individuals. Regularly, the law pronounces these unregistered grounds as saved or secured timberlands, or havens and national parks. The entrance of Tribal people group to woodland deliver or to the munching of cows is rendered unlawful; they are debilitated and punished for going into the backwoods. Countless individuals have a place with the Tribal people group. They experience each day under the erratic risk of being expelled from their homes; the main legitimate security they have is the due procedure of law. Throughout the years, when these individuals have challenged abuse by the woods office or raised their voices to request lawful rights, the State has utilized compel to smother themto the degree of denying them the privilege to life.

The National Forest Policy of 1988 perceives advantageous relationship amongst timberland and Tribal people group yet; the Tribal individuals have been efficiently misled under the Forest Act of 1927. At the point when the Forest Conservation Act of 1980 came into execution, a great many sections of land of place where there is Tribal people group were infringed overnight. In 2006, the legislature of India brought the Scheduled Tribes and Other Traditional Forest Dwellers Act. The Act is gone for fixing the deep rooted bad form done to Tribal people group by reestablishing and perceiving their previous rights (Tipper, 2014). The acknowledgment and rebuilding has been, however going through unpleasant climate in regard of its usage. The Government of India till today has neglected to tell the Rules of Procedures of the Forest Rights Act of 2006. In the in the meantime, Tribals keep on being arraigned for getting to minor timberland deliver. There were 2,57,226 timberland bodies of evidence pending against 1,62,692 Tribal people group in the vicinity of 1955 and 30 June 2006 under various Sections of the Forest Act of 1927.

Policies of Tribal Community Development comes Disadvantages

Tribal individuals who constituted 8.6% of the aggregate populace of India according to 2011 evaluation additionally constituted 55.1% of the aggregate advancement extend prompted uprooted people up to 2010 because of mega formative ventures like enterprises, mining, dams, untamed life asylums, parks and preservation of nature, and so forth. Improvement ventures have turned out to be more tricky especially in Andhra Pradesh amid the most recent couple of decades. In this setting take the Polavaram dam, which is to be worked over the Godavari River which will dislodge around 400,000 individuals in the three states; Andhra Pradesh, Chhattisgarh and Orissa. Of them no less than 150,000 are Tribals especially powerless Tribal gatherings beyond all doubt as far as vocation and protection of particular social legacy are in stun and the rest for the most part Dalit's reliant on minor backwoods deliver for their occupation. Dislodging not just upsets the lives of the people and families concerned, additionally their whole groups and social orders. Much of the time, because of relocation, financial frameworks and group structures separates. Subsequently, Tribal people group are at the most reduced point in each financial marker. In addition, they are occasionally restored. As India's dynamic economy includes encourage assets, Tribal people group confront more uprooting. In the most recent three years, the National Policy on Resettlement and Rehabilitation for Project Affected Families of 2004 was revised twice in 2006 and 2007, yet neglected to address the issues of uprooted individuals. Tribal people group must oppose for their privilege and popularity based cognizant individuals ought to bolster them in this regard.

Language and Language Rights to Tribal Community

Tribal people group have been notable protect and advance their dialect and culture; despite the fact that Article 19(5) of the constitution expresses that a social or etymologist minority has the privilege to ration its dialect and culture. This implies Triblas as individual and gatherings have appropriate to utilize their own particular dialect, to rehearse their own particular culture, to concentrate their own particular history, convention and legacy and so forth. The state can't, by law, force upon them whatever other culture or dialect. While the state might not have authorized any dialect or culture on them, neither has it made any positive strides worth the name towards meeting this arrangement of the constitution. Or maybe, the means taken are a long way from being in consonance with the arrangements set down in the constitution. The stance that they received has perpetually been toward digestion into the dialect and culture of the real group, as opposed to insurance and advancement of the particular dialect and culture of the Tribal people group. Tutoring stretched out to Tribal people group for instance, has perpetually been made in the dialect of the overwhelming territorial group of the separate states or in English. The outcome is that Tribal people group is progressively losing learning of their own dialect and culture. In reality the advancement of dialect and culture has been left to Tribal people group themselves. However, due to absence of control over human, hierarchical and money related assets, the Tribal people group has not possessed the capacity to take powerful measures in this course. Just where such support has been made accessible in some shape or the other the Tribal people group has possessed the capacity to secure and shield their way of life.

PESA Act in India against Violation

To reinforce the constitutional provisions for safety of the Tribal communities, this important Panchayat PESA Act 1996, has been enacted in latest years. The act empowers the scheduled Tribes to protect and preserve the traditions and customs of the humans, their cultural identification, network resources and normal mode of dispute decision via the Gram Saba. Curiously, the provisions of the Panchayat Act infrequently discover its due area in latter and spirit. but, there are massive violations of the PESA Act, 1996, in mining and land acquisition within the Scheduled regions of Andhra Pradesh, Chhattisgarh, Jharkhand and Orissa. Clause four.e.(1) of the PanchayatsAct, 1996, offers that every GramSabha shall approve the plans, programmes and projects for social and monetary improvement before such plans, programmes and tasks are taken up for implementation. Once more, clause four. (i) Says that —the Gram Sabha or the Panchayat at the best level shall be consulted earlier than making the purchase of land within the Scheduled areas for development initiatives. And before resettling or rehabilitating humans laid low with such projects in the Scheduled areas, the actual planning and implementation of the tasks in the Scheduled regions shall be coordinated on the state stage‖. no matter the above provisions for the rights of the Tribal communities, no necessary initiations are taken up at some stage in any developmental project to take the opinion and consent of the GramSabha, which constitutes people's evaluations. The tips of Gram Sabha aren't made mandatory prior to granting prospecting license or mining rent in lots of instances. as an example in the case of Polavaram a multipurpose venture, Gram Sabhas are not conducted in villages and peoples consent has not been taken. This technique is neither followed in Andhra Pradesh nor within the neighboring states like Orissa and Chattisgarh. Even though this undertaking did no longer get environmental clearance, creation of venture has been initiated.The charter entrusts the Governor the project of ensuring peace and appropriate governance'in agenda five areas, with absolute powers over the country government toward this end. Governors were also required to put up an annual document to the Parliament, which become supposed to be an unbiased assessment on administration in schedule 5 areas. but, since the enactment of PESA, Governors have slowly but absolutely been neglecting their duties towards the regulation, and closer to the welfare of the Tribal groups.

Even The authorities of India has also did not materialize Tribal sub plan inside the nation.

Conclusion

Infringement of human rights makes numerous monetary and enthusiastic issues. It influences the nature and welfare of individuals, and makes many scatters. It is conceivable to envision the life odds of Tribal people group enhancing through the usage of useful measures alongside considering the rights concurred. Be that as it may, quiet on rights will dependably convey with it the threat of an arrival to paternalism and the treatment of an identifiable gathering of individuals as an issue' deserving of philanthropy, not as a gathering of people to whom society has obligations and obligations. The established certification, which oversees and secures the rights and sway of Tribal people group, require a prompt execution. Something else, this would prompt to a vanishing of the different Tribal people group from the human picture. The Tribal people group's power is in question by the mediation of non-tribes in their general vicinity. Consequently, there is a quick need to constitute Tribal independence committees so that the Tribal people group themselves can take care of the guidelines, execution and advancement of the areas.

References

1.   Aiyar Mani, S. 2002. *"Panchayati Raj: The Way Forward"*. Economic and Political Weekly, August 2002

2.   Baxi, Upendra. 2002. The Future of Human Rights. Oxford University Press, New Delhi.

3.   Krishna, Halvath. 2001. Human Rights and Realties of Tribals Live in India: A Perfect Storm. Vol-19, Issue-4, ISSN-2279-0845, pp-43-46.

4.   Minz, N. 1993. Cultural Identity of Tribals in India. *Social Action*, Vol. 43, Jan-March. Pp 32- 40.

5.   Nair, R. 2006. *Human Rights in India: Historical, Social and Political Perspectives*. New Delhi: Oxford University Press.

6.   Sachar, R. 2009. *Human Rights-Prospects & Challenges*. Gyan Publishing House, New Delhi.

7.   Sachar, R. 2009. *Human Rights: Prospects & Challenges*. Gyan Publishing House, New Delhi.

8.   Shah, G. 2004. *Social Movements in India: A Review of literature*. Sage Publications, New Delhi.

9.   Sharma B.D. 2010. *"Report of the sub-committee appointed"* by the Ministry of Panchayati Raj to draft Model Guidelines to vest Gram Sabhas with powers as envisaged in PESA'

10.   Thipper, B.2014. Right over forest land for Tribals in the offing, The Indian Express, P. 6

CHAPTER
15

HUMAN RIGHT FOR MINORITIES IN INDIAN CONSTITUTION

Dr. Munesh Kumar
Assistant Professor
Government Law College,
Churu
(Rajasthan)

Introduction

The task of drafting a Constitution with the aim of promoting common good and also satisfying the aspirations and allaying the apprehensions of minorities in a communally charged environment was indeed a difficult assignment at the time of Independence that accompanied partition of the country along communal lines. However, the framers of the Constitution demonstrated perspicacity and vision in preparing a document that meets both the ends of achieving national unity while respecting diversities. The most striking features of the Constitution in this respect are the secularism along with democratic egalitarianism and fundamental rights with special and additional safeguards for weaker sections of society like Scheduled Castes, Scheduled Tribes, the Other Backward Classes and minorities. As India is a conglomeration of minorities, the Constitution has taken special care of them.

The starting point of discussion on incorporation of minority rights in the Indian Constitution was the Objectives Resolution moved by Pandit Jawaharlal Nehru in the Constituent Assembly on 13 December 1946. The Resolution guaranteed to all the people of India Justice— social, economic and political; equality of status, opportunity, and before the law; freedom of thought, expression, belief, faith, worship, vocation, association and action subject to law and public morality. It also promised adequate safeguards for minorities, backward and tribal areas, and depressed and other backward classes. In this way, the Objectives Resolution which broadly outlined the basic framework and philosophy of the Constitution gave assurances to apprehensive minorities that their interests would be safeguarded by the Constitution. Thereafter/ the Constituent Assembly created an Advisory Committee on Fundamental Rights and Minorities etc. under the Chairmanship of Sardar Vallabh Bhai Patel. This Committee appointed a Sub-Committee on Minorities with H.C. Mookherjee as its Chairman. This Sub-Committee on Minorities began its work with a questionnaire prepared and distributed by K.M. Munshi. The questionnaire included questions on political and economic safeguards for the minorities and creation of a body or appointment of officer for looking after the affairs of minorities in the light of constitutional guarantees given to them. The deliberations on rights of minorities passed through three stages:

First Stage: Rejection of separate electorates and adoption of joint electorates with reservation of seats for the minorities and Scheduled Castes in legislative bodies and public services.

Second Stage: Rejection of joint electorates with reservation of seats for minorities in legislative bodies and general agreement on reservation of minorities and Scheduled Castes in Public Services.

Third Stage: Denial of reservations to the minorities while reaffirming reservations for the Scheduled Castes and Scheduled Tribes in Public employment and legislative bodies and recognition of the religious, educational cultural and linguistic rights of minorities.

As emphasized above it is of fundamental importance that the minority is protected against discrimination and exploitation. In this context it is significant to note that the Indian Constitution as well as the International legal regime have recognized the same and have accorded them a special status. Free India addressed itself to the formulation of human rights through the legal instrument of the Constitution. The human rights content of the Indian Constitution is a complex amalgam of civil and political rights, economic rights, religious rights, minority rights etc. The Right of Equality (Art. 14, 15 and 16) and the Right to live (Art.21) are the most important of the general rights. Article 14 enshrines the broad right of equality whereas Art. 15 and 16 are more specific in nature, the former prohibition the state from discriminating against any citizen on grounds only of religion, cast, sex, race, place of birth or any of them and the latter mandating equality of opportunity in matters of public employment. Article 21 is said to be the fountainhead of all the rights conferred under the Constitution. It provides that no person shall be deprived of his life or personal liberty except according to the procedure established by law. The Indian Courts have in their wisdom widened the scope and ambit to bring within Article 21 many of the well established norms of human rights.

The United Nations General Assembly unanimously passed the International Covenant on Civil and Political Rights. Article 27 of the same runs as follows-

"In those States in which ethnic, religious or linguistic minorities exist, persons belonging to such minorities shall not be denied the right, in community with other members of their group, to enjoy their own culture to profess and practice their own religion, or to use their own language."

The Indian Constitution had already granted these to its citizens vide Article 25 to 30. Article 25, 26, 27 and 28 embody the right to profess and practice their own religion. Article 29 gives the right to minorities to conserve their own distinct language, script or culture. Article 30 provides the right to establish and administer educational institutions of their choice. Thus, it is very clear that as far as the letter of the law is concerned the rights of the minorities are well protected.

Thus, we find that the Constituent Assembly in the beginning started discussion on minority rights with a very positive and generous approach. The members of the Assembly were deliberating upon providing special rights to minorities to ensure their meaningful political representation, social and economic security besides agreeing on preserving their religious, cultural and educational rights. However, ultimately no special rights except cultural and educational rights were conceded to minorities whereas the reservations for the Scheduled Castes and Scheduled Tribes in legislative bodies and public employment were kept intact. Perhaps the Constitution finally adopted by the Constituent Assembly on 26 November 1949 took into consideration the heterogeneous character of the people and resolved to establish a new social order based on secularism and to recognize cultural and linguistic differences within the framework of political and economic unity of the nation. Nevertheless, it cannot be contested that denial of reservations to the minorities in public employment and central and provincial legislature was nonetheless a devastating blow to their socio-economic and political interests.

The Constitution of India is a classic example of accommodation and adjustment of the claims of various groups and communities inhabiting this country. The minorities derive their rights from the Constitution in many ways. There is varying nature of minority rights in the Constitution. There are ideals expressed in the Preamble, which directly or indirectly affect minority rights. There are Fundamental Rights of general nature available to all citizens of the country but these rights also protect minorities from oppression and discrimination. These individual rights available to all are legally justifiable and therefore implemented by the executive and the judiciary very forcefully. Besides, there are some Fundamental Rights specifically dealing with the problems of minorities. In fact, these rights are embodied in Articles 29 and 30. The intention of the framers of the Constitution in the beginning was to protect the educational, cultural and linguistic rights of minorities through these provisions. Nevertheless,, the changes made after the Partition rendered the safeguards very weak. The apparent conflict between Articles 29(2) and 30(1) has made the cultural and education rights of minorities a victim of judicial misinterpretation in many cases. As the Constitution of India was deliberately made at a particular juncture of our national history, many problems faced by the nation were not foreseen by the framers of the Constitution. Thus, since 1950, the Constitution has been constantly evolving and amendments are being made according to the exigencies of the time. Hence, the rights of minorities must be restored through this evolutionary process and as the judiciary has played a commendable role in giving harmonious interpretation to the letter and spirit of our Constitution, it must look into the matter of rights of minorities in the similar fashion in consonance with the secular and democratic spirit of the Constitution. There is a pressing need to remove the contradictions or conflict between Articles 29(2) and 30(1) so that the only specific rights conceded to minorities may be implemented in their true letter and spirit.

Other provisions of the Constitution are also important for minorities but what can be safely assumed is that the rights provided to minorities are proving to be inadequate in present circumstances. Not only the various provision relating to minorities are to be enforced with strong political will in their true letter and spirit but also certain new provisions and safeguards are needed for the protection of their interests. The socio-economic and educational backwardness of the minorities calls for immediate special measures by the Government of India. The Muslim minority in particular is very backward in comparison to all other communities, which is evident from the report of the Sachar Committee. It has been rightly observed in the Report that in a pluralistic society a reasonable representation of various communities in government sector employment is necessary to enhance participatory governance. While legislating on rights of minorities or pronouncing judgements on minority rights, it is suggested that the current discourse on minorities in the United Nations and at other international for a may be taken into account. The Constitutional law of India must reflect the spirit of international jurisprudence on minority rights.

References

1.	"Who are minorities in India?" See hhtps://crative. sulek hna.com-322941-blog.

2.	Ansari, Iqbal A. Readings on Minorities, Perspectives and Documents, Vol. II, Institute of Objective Studies. New Delhi, PP. XXXII-XXXIV.

3.	Basu, D.D. 1997. Introduction to the Constitution of India, Prentice Hall of India, New Delhi.

4.	Chandhoke, Neera. 1999. *Beyond Secularism, The Rights of Religious Minorities*. Oxford University Press, New Delhi.

5.	Church of God (Full Gospel) in India v. K. K. R. Majestic Colony. Welfare Association, AIR 2000 SC 2773.

6.	Constituent Assembly Debates [CAD], Vol. I.

7.	Engineer, Asghar Ali. 1999. *"Media and Minorities:*

Exclusions, Distortions and Stereotypes", Economic and Political Weekly, 34(31).

8. https://www.minorityrights.org/5648/india-overview.html

9. Prime Minister's High Level Committee on Social, Economic and Educational Status of the Muslim Community of India (Sachar Committee), 2006.

10. Rao, B. Shiva. 1968. *The Framing of India's Constitution, Select Documents*, Vol. II, N.M. Tripathi, Bombay.

11. Religion conflicts in India. 2016. Retrieved from http://www.en.wikipedia.org/wiki/religious_conflicts_in-india.

12. Sarkar, Sukanta. 2015. *Human Rights Violations of Minorities*. Anmol Publications Pvt. Ltd. New Delhi.

13. Sheoram, Chandra Pal. 1994. *"Minority Rights under the Constitution: Emerging issues"*, Kashmir University Laxu Review, Vol. 1.

14. Yaqin, Anwarul. "Educational and Cultural Rights of Minorities under the Indian Constitution Drafting History of Articles 29 and 30", in Iqbal A. Ansari (ed.), op. cit, Vol. III.

CHAPTER 16

HUMAN RIGHTS EDUCATION- INDIA AND INTERNATIONAL

Ram Kumar Verma
Assistant Professor
J.B.T.T. B.Ed. College,
23PTP, Sadulshahar
(Sri Ganganagar)

Introduction

The right to education is recognised, promoted and protected at all levels from national, regional to international. Education is the primary vehicle by which economically and socially marginalised adults and children can lift themselves out of poverty and obtain the means to participate fully in their communities. Education has a vital role in empowering women, safeguarding children from exploitative and hazardous labor and sexual exploitation, promoting human rights and democracy, protecting the environment, and controlling population growth. Several international conventions, numerous writings and reports by United Nations (UN) bodies stress the importance of the fundamental right to education. The right to education is a fundamental human right. It is also central to realizing other human rights. Education is an extraordinary tool of empowerment. It is essential for the promotion and protection of all human rights. However, too often at both the national and international levels not enough is done to ensure the effective implementation of the right to education. Achieving the right to basic education, as a fundamental human right, is one of the biggest development challenges faced by the international community today. Millions of children, youth and adults remain deprived of basic education

The Right to Receive an Education

At international level the ICESCR devotes two articles to the right to education, namely, Articles 13 and 14. Article 13 contains the longest provision in the ICESCR, and is the most wide-ranging and comprehensive article on the right to education in international human rights law. According to Article 13(1) of the ICESCR, states parties agree that all education, whether public or private, formal or non-formal, shall be directed towards the aims and objectives identified in Article13 (1). Interpreted in the light of the World Declaration on Education for All, the Convention on the Rights of the Child, the Vienna Declaration and Programmed of Action, and the Plan of Action for the United Nations Decade for Human Rights Education. While all these texts closely correspond to Article 13(1) of the ICESCR, they also include elements, which are not expressly provided for in Article 13(1), such as specific references to gender equality and respect for the environment. These new elements are implicit in and reflect a contemporary interpretation of

Article 13(1).

Principle of Non-Discrimination

The fundamental obligation in the ICESCR is for the states parties to "take steps" towards realising the rights enumerated in the ICESCR. This obligation allows a great deal of scope for states to determine the measures they adopt in order to implement the ICESCR. Article 2(2) places special importance on legislative measures, but it clearly also envisages other measures which might include judicial, administrative, financial, educational and social implementation. Consequently, a lack of legislative measures does not necessarily entail a failure to implement the obligations imposed by the ICESCR because alternative measures may suffice and, indeed, in some circumstances, may be more appropriate. Nevertheless, some legislative measures will usually be necessary. Furthermore, legislative means may be desirable because their public nature leaves them open to effective scrutiny

The Right to Primary Education

According to Article 13(2)(a) of the ICESCR, primary education shall be compulsory and free to all. Primary education includes the elements of availability, accessibility, acceptability and adaptability, which are common to education in all its forms and at all levels. The Committee took guidance on the proper interpretation of the term "primary education" from the World Declaration on Education for All which states: "The main delivery system for the basic education of children outside the family is primary schooling."Primary education must be universal, ensure that the basic learning needs of all children are satisfied, and take into account the culture, needs and opportunities of the community. The Declaration further defines "basic learning needs" as "essential learning tools, such as literacy, oral expression, numeracy, and problem solving and the basic learning content such as knowledge, skills, values, and attitudes required by human beings to be able to survive, to develop their full capacities, to live and work in dignity, to participate fully in development, to improve the quality of their lives, to make informed decisions, and to continue learning". While primary education is not synonymous with basic education, there is a close correspondence between the two. As formulated in Article 13(2)(a), primary education has two distinctive features: it is "compulsory" and "available free to all". The element of compulsion serves to highlight the fact that neither parents, nor guardians, nor the state are entitled to treat as optional the decision as to whether the child should have access to primary education. The nature of this requirement is unequivocal. The right is expressly formulated so as to ensure the availability of primary education without charge to the child, parents or guardians. Fees imposed by the government, the local authorities or the school, and other direct costs, constitute disincentives to the enjoyment of the right and may jeopardise its realisation.

The Right to Secondary Education

Article 13(2)(b) applies to secondary education "in its different forms", thereby recognising that secondary education demands flexible curricula and varied delivery systems to respond to the needs of students in different social and cultural settings. According to Article 13(2)(b), secondary education "shall be made generally available and accessible to all by every appropriate means, and in particular by the progressive introduction of free education". The phrase "generally available" signifies, firstly, that secondary education is not dependent on a student's apparent capacity or ability and, secondly, that secondary education will be transmitted throughout the state in such a way that it is available on the same basis to all. Progressive introduction of free education means that while states must priorities the provision of free primary education, they also have an obligation to take concrete steps towards achieving free secondary and higher education.

The Right to Higher Education

Article 13(2)(c) is formulated on the same lines as Article 13(2)(b). There are three differences between the two provisions. Article 13(2)(c) does not include a reference to either education "in its different forms" or specifically to TVE. The third and most significant difference between Article 13(2)(b) and (c) is that while secondary education "shall be made generally available and accessible to all", higher education "shall be made equally accessible to all, on the basis of capacity". These two omissions reflect only a difference of emphasis between Article 13(2)(b) and (c). If higher education is to respond to the needs of students in different social and cultural settings, it must have flexible curricula and varied delivery systems, such as distance learning; in practice, therefore, both secondary and higher education have to be available "in different forms The third and most significant difference between Article 13(2)(b) and (c) is that while secondary education "shall be made generally available and accessible to all", higher education "shall be made equally accessible to all, on the basis of capacity".

The Right to Fundamental Education

By virtue of Article 13(2)(d), individuals "who have not received or completed the whole period of their primary education" have a right to fundamental education, or basic education as defined in the World Declaration on Education For All. Since everyone has the right to the satisfaction of their "basic learning needs" as understood by the World Declaration, the right to fundamental education is not confined to those "who have not received or completed the whole period of their primary education". The right to fundamental education extends to all those who have not yet satisfied their "basic learning needs". Fundamental education, therefore, is an integral component of adult education and life-long learning. Because fundamental education is a right of all age groups, curricula and delivery systems must be devised which are suitable for students of all ages.

Principle of Compulsory Education Free of Charge for All

Article 14 of the ICESCR requires that each state party which has not been able to secure compulsory primary education free of charge should adopt within two years a detailed plan of action for the progressive implementation of such. In spite of this obligation a number of states parties have neither drafted nor implemented a plan of action for free and compulsory primary education. This obligation is a continuing one and states parties to which the provision is relevant by virtue of the prevailing situation are not absolved from the obligation as a result of their past failure to act within the two-year limit. The plan must cover all of the actions which are necessary in order to secure each of the requisite component parts of the right, and must be sufficiently detailed so as to ensure the comprehensive realisation of the right. The right to education, recognised in Articles 13 and 14 of the ICESCR, as well as in a variety of other international treaties, such as the Convention on the Rights of the Child and the Convention on the Elimination of All Forms of Discrimination against Women,Plans of action prepared by states parties to the ICESCR in accordance with Article 14 are especially important as the work of the Committee has shown that the lack of educational opportunities for children often reinforces their subjection to various other human rights violations. For instance, these children, who may live in abject poverty and not lead healthy lives, are particularly vulnerable to forced labour and other forms of exploitation. is of vital importance.

Right to Education Jurisprudence in India

In India the judiciary has shown its deep concern for providing free and compulsory education to all children below the age of 14 years. The right to free primary education has now been declared as a fundamental right by the Indian Supreme Court. The theory of the complementary nature of rights declared in Part III and Part IV and the harmonious interpretation of these rights has been the foundation for the realisation of primary education being declared a fundamental right today in India. The Supreme Court of India in the Bandhua Mukti Morcha. The issue of the scope and extent of right to education came up before the Supreme Court in Mohini Jain case held that the right to education is implicit in and flows from the right to life guaranteed by Article 21. That the right to education has been treated as one of transcendental importance in the life of an individual has been recognised not only in this country since thousands of years, but all over the world.

Education Policy in India

With a view to realising the constitutional goals set for education, the government of India in 1964 appointed the Education Commission (1964–1966). The Commission was entrusted with the task of evolving a national system of education. It recommended a radical transformation in the prevailing education system and highlighted the need for the "common school approach" to promote equity and social justice. The first National Policy on Education (NPE), 1968 recommended free and compulsory elementary education and equalisation of educational opportunities especially for girls and children belonging to SCs and STs. Another National Policy on Education (NPE–1986) was adopted and further updated in 1992. The NPE 1986 provides for a comprehensive policy framework for the development of education up to the end of the century and a Plan of Action (POA) 1992, assigning specific responsibilities for organising, implementing and financing its proposals

Right to Education at Primary Level in India

For the first time in the history of education in India a Department for Primary Education has been opened in the Ministry of Human Resource Development at New Delhi. A new primary education policy has been launched under the scheme of Sarva Shiksha Abhiyan (SSA) at the district level throughout the country in 2001.The assistance under the programme of SSA was on the basis of an 85 to 15 ratio sharing arrangement between the central government and the state government during the Ninth Plan, and at a 75 to 25 ratio during the Tenth Plan, and at 50 to 50 ratio thereafter. 'Draft Education Bill Upsets Schools', Times of India, 17 December 2005. The programme covers the entire country, except the State of Goa. The Ministry has also set up a National Mission for SSA under the chairmanship of the prime minister. The first meeting of the Governing Council of National Mission was held on 21 February 2005. The planned allocations for elementary education have increased steadily but are still not quite adequate to fulfill the constitutional commitments. The period following the adoption of National Policy on Education (NPE) 1986 saw the introduction of a number of centrally sponsored schemes to cater to the specific needs of the elementary education sector.

Right to Education at Higher Level in India

The NPE 1986 underscores adult education for the eradication of illiteracy, particularly in the age group of 15–35. A vast programme of adult and continuing education was implemented through various ways and channels, including the establishment of centres in rural areas for continuing education. A number of programmes taken up to impart adult education during the last four decades before launching of the National Literacy Mission in May 1988 could not be very successful on account of a number of inherent weaknesses such as the low levels of literacy, centre-based approach, lack of mass awareness and community participation. However, the government of India continues to pursue the mass literacy mission, which ultimately brought encouraging results. The number of illiterates during the decade 1991–2001 came down from 329 million in 1991 to 304 million in 2001. This was a welcome change in the depressing scenario. The scheme of continuing education provides a learning continuum to the efforts of Total Literacy and Post-Literacy Programmes in the country. The main thrust is on providing further learning opportunities to neo-literates by setting up Continuing Education Centres (CECs) and Nodal Continuing Education Centres (NCECs), to serve a population of about 2000–2500 people by providing facilities of libraries, reading rooms, learning centres, sports and cultural centres and other individual interest promotion programmes. As a part of this strategy, there is stress on establishing rural libraries, which will provide reading and learning material to neo-literates in their own languages. Wide acceptance of this programme is achieved by involving non-governmental organisations, voluntary agencies, social workers, and Panchayati Raj institutions in the planning and implementation of the scheme of continuing education. Various development departments, technical institutions, professional groups and the Directorate of Adult Education, Government of India provide the input needed by the programme. State Resource Centres (SRCs) and Jan Shikshan Sansthans join hands by giving the necessary resource and training support. The social mobilisation generated by the literacy campaigns has had an enormous impact on other social sectors, most notably women's empowerment, health and population stabilisation along with environmental awareness. A framework for effective social action has been provided by the Panchayati Raj Institutions. The campaigns have served the cause of promoting equity and social justice in society and fostering of a scientific temper and a sense of belonging to India's great composite culture and consciousness of unity in diversity.

Conclusion

The ICESCR provides for progressive realisation and acknowledges the constraints due to the limits of available resources. It also imposes on states parties various obligations which are of immediate effect. States have a specific and continuing obligation "to move as expeditiously and effectively as possible" towards the full realisation of Article 13. States parties must closely monitor education including all relevant policies, institutions, programmes, spending patterns and other practices so as to identify and take measures to redress any de facto discrimination. Education operates as a multiplier, enhancing the enjoyment of all individual rights and freedoms where the right to education is effectively guaranteed, while depriving people of the enjoyment of many rights and freedoms where the right to education is denied or violated.

In the last 60 years the government of India has evolved very successful programmes in imparting primary education in the country. Primary education is now provided in the mother tongue or regional language in all the states and union territories (UTs). There has been substantial increase in access to elementary education, with reduced class, caste and sectional disparities. Despite substantial achievements, the task of universal elementary education (UEE) is far from complete. Enrolments in the schools have certainly increased but so have the number of out of school children. Sadly, the country today has one of the largest illiterate populations in the world. Caste, gender, class and regional disparities in UEE though reduced are still glaring and persistent. The educational administration in most states and UTs has yet to effectively tackle endemic problems concerning shortage of teachers, teacher absenteeism, inadequate and improperly designed school buildings, lack of teaching/learning equipment, need-based teacher training, and a curriculum related to real life requirements.

Reference

1. Chand, Attar.1985. "Politics of Human Rights and Civil Liberties - A Global Survey". UDH Publishers, Delhi.pp-45.

2. Encyclopedia of Human Rights Issues since 1945

3. Encyclopedia of Human Rights by David P. Forsythe (editor)

4. Human and Civil Rights hyperlink "https://ez.lib.jjay.cuny.edu/login?url=https://go.galegroup.com/ps/i.do?id=FALE%7C9781414412627&v=2.1&u=cuny_main&it=aboutbook&p=GVRL&sw=w"

5. Human Rights: A Reference Handbook by Nina Redman, Lucille Whalen

6. Nehru, Jawaharlal. *The Discovery of India*". 2nd ed. (New Delhi. Jawaharlal Nehru Memorial Fund, 1992) 88.

7. Radhakrishnan, S. 1958. *'The Bhagavadgita*". (George Allen and Unv., London .pp-276.

8. Singh, Nagendra. 1986. *Enforcement of Human Rights*". Eastern Law House Pvt. Ltd, Calcutta. Pp-7.

9. The Human Rights Encyclopedia

10. Tyagi, Yogesh K. 1981. "*Third World Response to Human Rights*". Indian Journal of International Law, Vo.21, No.1 (January -March 1981): pp.120-121.

CHAPTER
17

HUMAN RIGHTS AND ONLINE SHOPPING BEHAVIOUR

Ms. Charmaine D'souza
Associate Professor
Department of Commerce,
Rosary College,
Navelim,
Salcete -GOA

Introduction

You have the right to information about everything that you pay for. Every customer has the right to know the price, weight, quantity and quality of the goods and services for which he is paying to know that he is not being misled by the unfair trade practices. Every consumer has the right to be protected against any sale of the product or service which is dangerous to life. The right to be educated on consumer protectionwhich ensures thatproper informational programs are in place that are easily accessible and help consumers make purchasing decisions andhave the Right to Seek Redressal. Consumers also have the right to be heard in consumer courts or forums that deal with dispute cases. Organizations in such industries should operate in a responsible manner, complying with applicable legal requirements and with respect for human rights, local communities, and the environment. The internet has played a significant role in our daily life in that people can talk globally, send email around the clock, search information, and even can buy things online. (Bourlakis et al., 2008). It provides consumer more information and choices to compare product and price, more choice, convenience, easier to find anything online (Butler and Peppard, 1998). Online shopping has been shown to provide more satisfaction to modern consumers seeking convenience and speed (Yu and Wu, 2007). Online shopping is the process whereby consumers directly buy goods or services from a seller in real-time, without an intermediary service, over the Internet and the sale or purchase transaction is completed electronically.[1] Online shopping is gaining a lot of popularity as everything is made available at our door steps, which saves a lot of time and effort and also helps us to avoid a lot of inconvenience involved in travelling to a conventional store and can be reached at any time, as they operate 24 hours.[2] Now a days, the more involvement of companies in online shopping mode provides the various benefits to the customers like less cost, more discounts, fast delivery, better quality, combo offers, replacement facility, guarantee and warrantee of products, discount coupons on next purchase and many more.[3]

Motivations that lead consumer to buy online can be summarized into four categories-convenience, information, available products and services, and cost and time efficiency. Empirical research shows that convenient of the internet is one of the impacts on consumers' willingness to buy online

(Wang et al.,2005). Online shopping is available for customers around the clock comparing to traditional store as it is open 24 hours a day, 7 days a week (Wang et al., 2005).Research shows that 58% chose to shop online because they could shop after-hours, when the traditional stores are closed and 61% of the respondents selected to shop online because they want to avoid crowds and wailing lines, especially in holiday shopping (The Tech Faq,2008). The internet has made the data accessing easier (Wang et al., 2005). Given customers rarely have a chance to touch and feel product and service online before they make decision, online sellers normally provide more product information that customers can use when making a purchase (Lim and Dubinsky, 2004). Customers put the weight on the information that meets their information needs (Kenny's, 1999). In addition to get information from its website, consumers can also benefit from products' reviews by other customers. They can read those reviews before they make a decision. It gives customers chances to compare price from different websites and find the products with lower prices some websites, Ebay for example, offer customers auction or best offer option, so they can make a good deal for their product makes shopping a real game of chance and treasure hunt and makes shopping a fun and entertainment.

Thus, the purpose of this study is to identify factors affecting Indian consumers' attitude toward shopping online. Also, potential gender difference in identifying factors affecting male/female purchase behaviour was investigated.

In the online shopping context, the level of perceived risk may be magnified due to limited physical access to products and sales personnel (Forsythe and Shi 2003); thereby discouraging shoppers from purchasing via the Internet [Forsythe & Shi 2003; Garbarino and Strahilevitz 2004]. Bhatnagar and Ghose (2004) argued that product risk has the most significant negative impact on shoppers' online purchase intentions. However, Eggert (2006) found that compared to product risk, perceptions of privacy risk have greater impact on willingness to purchase on the Internet. Among relevant risk dimensions associated with shopping in general identified in traditional channels [Jacoby and Kaplan 1972; Peter and Tarpey 1975], product and financial risks have shown significant negative influences on shoppers' Internet purchase intentions (Bhatnagar and Ghose 2004; Lu et al. 2005).

Product risk or performance risk: is defined as the probability of the item failing to meet the performance requirements originally intended (Peter and Tarpey 1975). *Financial risk*: is defined as the likelihood of suffering a monetary loss from a purchase Horton 1984; *Privacy risk:* is defined as the probability of having personal information disclosed as a result of online transactions Garbarino and Strahilevitz 2004; *Delivery risk*: Potential loss of delivery associated with goods lost, goods damaged and sent to the wrong place after shopping (Dan et al., 2007). *Social risk*: refers to the perception that a product purchased may result in disapproval by family or friends.[4]

Review of Literature

Bhattacharya et.al., (2004) -, found that individuals tend to purchase less through the internet because the online payment for internet shopping involves risk and online shopping involves longer delivery time.

Curtis., (2000) - highlights that people tend to browse and surf the internet more for information than for online shopping.

Delafrooz et al., (2009) - studied that consumers who highly evaluate the utilitarian aspect of shopping will more likely use the internet as an information source.

Jun et al., (2011) - studied that online consumers apparently want to receive the right quality and right quantity of items that they have ordered within the time frame, promised by the retailers, and they expect to be billed accurately.

Lee et al., (2003) – studied perceived risk is extremely important to understand the online shopping behaviour because it impacts other consumer perceptions

Nagra & Gopal., (2013) - reveals that on-line shopping in India is significantly affected by various Demographic factors like age, gender, marital status, family size and income.

Research Methodology

The data for the purpose of study was collected both from primary sources and secondary sources. A combination of Interview method and Questionnaire method was used to collect data from the respondents. A total of 200 respondents were interviewed using the questionnaire to understand the perception of customers towards online shopping .The constructs measured in the questionnaire followed five-point likert scale ranging fromStrongly Disagree (1), Disagree (2), Neutral (3), Agree (4) and Strongly Agree (5).

Secondary data to was collected for the purpose of study.

The sources included journals and websites.

Sample Design

The method of random sampling was used to collect data from the respondents.

Sample Size

A total of 200 respondents in rural, urban and semi urban parts of South-Goa having different age and income groups were pooled together to achieve the objectives of the study.

Statistical Tool

In data analysis and interpretation method of "chi-square test" and K-S one sample test were used to analyse the data. Also other tools such as percentage analysis, simple charting and tabulation were used to understand the behaviour of the respondents for online shopping.

Questionnaire Development

In the present study a questionnaire was prepared which included three sub-sections. The first part was the demographic profile of respondents, while the second part was a likert scale and third section, generalized on online shopping.

Table 1: Gender

Gender	Percentage of Respondents
Male	36
Female	64

Source: Primary Data

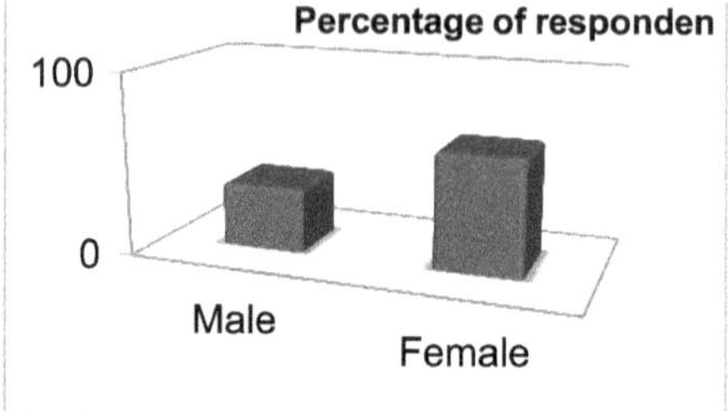

Source: Primary Data

From table 1 we can see that 36% of the respondents in the sample are male and the rest were female (i.e. 64%).A majority of 62.5% of the respondents are graduates, 22.5% have done their HSSC (12th), about 8.5%have completed their SSC while a minority of 6.5%hold a Post-Graduation (PG) degree.

Table 2: Problems of Online ShoppingChart 2: Problems of Online Shopping

Problems of online shopping	Percentage of respondents
Delayed delivery	26.5
Cheap quality products	11.5
Damage	19.5
Non-delivery	21
No problem	21.5

Source: Primary Data

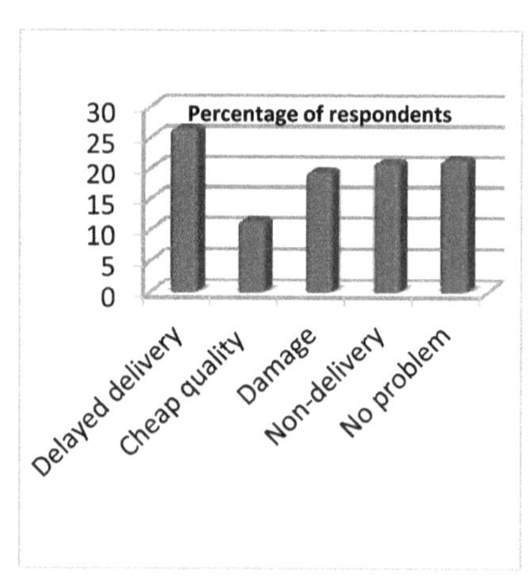

Source: Primary Data

The bar diagram clearly shows that (26.5%) of the respondents had the problem with delayed in the delivery. (21.5%) of the people agree that they face no problem in online shopping, while (21%) of them had to face problem with the non-delivery of the product. A very few (11.5%) respondents don't prefer to shop online due to quality concern.

CHI-SQUARE DISTRIBUTION

The test is applied when the data have two categorical variables from a single population. It is used to determine whether there is a significant association between the two variables.

➢ To measure the relationship between the gender and monthly income of the respondents.

$$\chi^2 = \left(\frac{O_1 - E_1}{E_1}\right)^2 + \left(\frac{O_2 - E_2}{E_2}\right)^2 + \cdots + \left(\frac{O_n - E_n}{E_n}\right)^2$$

Where, Degrees of freedom (Df) = (r -1) (c-1)

Level of significance (L.O.S.) = 5% (0.05)

Table 3: Perception of Online Shoppers to his Age and Gender

Gender	Age				Total
	<18	19-25	26-35	36>	
Male	2	38	25	7	**72**
Female	2	101	16	9	**128**
Total	**4**	**138**	**41**	**16**	**200**

Source: Primary Data

To test whether the age and gender have significant impact on online shopping, chi-square test is conducted.

H_0: Gender is independent of the age of the respondents.

H_1: Gender is not independent on the age of the respondents.

	Value	Df	p-value
Chi-Square	16.384	3	0.0009

The analysis reveals that the calculated value is 16.384 as the p-value is found to be 0.0009.hence the p-value is less than 0.05 degree of error there is significant difference between age and gender of the respondents.

Table 4: Perceived Risk in Online Shopping

Perceived risk	1	2	3	4	5
Social risk	10.25	12.75	32.25	33.5	11.25
Delivery risk	4.5	10.67	32.67	33.67	18.5
Financial risk	6.7	9.33	30.5	39.83	13.67
Privacy risk	5.5	11.25	32	37.25	14
Product risk	6.75	9	33.5	33.25	17.5

Source: Primary data
(1=Strongly Disagree, 2=Disagree, 3=Neutral, 4=Agree, 5=Strongly Agree)

The respondents expressed their opinion towards perceived risk in online shopping and it was noted that 41.3% respondents strongly disagreed that social risk has a greater impact on online shopping, 15.3% respondents strongly agreed that social risk is of a great importance in online shopping. 20% were neutral in their response as they didn't havemuch impact on them, 14.7% strongly disagreed that delivery risk in online shopping do not affect them, and when asked about financial risk in online shopping 22.5% agreed that it affect them, 13.3 % strongly disagreed that it does not make much difference to them. Privacy is very important to every consumer we see that 22.7% respondents feel that internet does not affect their privacy and while 14.7% feels that payment made online is secure. 22.9% respondentsare neutral in their response for product risk in online shopping, while 16% strongly disagree that product ordered online are not of good quality.

Kolmogorov –Smirnov (K-S) one sample test

The one sample Kolmogorov-Smirnov test is used to test whether a sample comes from a specific distribution. We can use this procedure to determine whether a sample comes from a population which is normally distributed.

Steps in the K-S one sample analysis:

1. We hypothesize about the population by stating the null and alternate hypothesis the null hypothesis would be

HO: Respondents falling under each category is same.

H1: Respondents falling under each category is not same.

2.   We calculate the observed and expected frequency (in proportion) for each category of the scale.

3.   Calculate the cumulative, observed and expected proportion. We calculate the K-S statistics that is D value. D value is basically absolute difference between the cumulative observed and expected proportion for all the categories of

Scale. Identify the largest absolute difference that is D_{max}.

Therefore the D_{max} is the highest difference between the observed and expected proportion.

4.   We compare the D_{max} value the critical value D critical and make a decision for null hypothesis. If the $D_{max} > D_{critical}$, we reject the null hypothesis.

The critical value would be
$D_{critical} = 1.36 / \sqrt{n}$ where; n is sample size (200)

Table 5: K-S one Sample Test

Criteria	$D_{critical}$	D_{max}	Decision
Timeconsciousness			
Browsing on the internet saves a lot of my window time.	0.096	0.275	Reject H_o
Shopping in the local markets is time consuming and problematic.	0.096	0.245	Reject H_o

Price consciousness			
The quality of products purchased online from trusted sites is very good and are available at economical prices.	0.096	0.235	Reject H_o
Online shopping provides the possibility of price comparison.	0.096	0.28	Reject H_o

As $D_{max} > D_{critical}$, we reject the null hypothesis.

Since the calculated D_{max} is greater than $D_{critical}$, the null hypothesis of significant difference among the customers' perception towards time consciousness and price consciousness, the satisfaction levels cannot be rejected. It is evident that there is significant difference between the satisfaction levels of the customers. We can very well infer from the data that majority of the customers are highly satisfied by the time consciousness and price consciousness in online shopping.

Conclusion

The entire evolution of e-commerce has happened over last 15-16 years withmore than 200 million internet users in India , with approximately 89 million users visiting online shopping sites.[5]Lack of trust, for instance, seems to be the major reason that impedes consumers to buy online. This study was accomplished to determine the customer behaviour of South Goa towards online shopping. In this research we have seen the behaviour of the consumers towards various factors like risk, characteristics. Although the risk seemed to be the only factor significantly affecting Indian consumers online purchases, when looking at male and female perceptions, there are different factors affecting male/female consumer behaviour. Overall the use of internet as a shopping channel, tends to generate shopping demand because of the unpredicted large amount of product information available online and the direct impact of online buying on stores.[6] India has the explosive growth of 354 million usersin internet usage has recently led to a corresponding growth in online business and ecommerce. This growth presents both great opportunities as well as some challenges.[7] Online shopping has become extremely popular over the last decade. Use of technology has opened new doors and opportunities that enable a convenient lifestyle today.[8] At present the market is estimated at Rs 46,000 crores and is growing at 100 per cent per year.[9]

4.2 Findings

In our study regarding online shopping behaviour of customers in South-Goa the following are the findings given below:

➤   64% are of the respondents are females and 36% are males.

➤   Majority (69.5%) of the respondents belong to the age group of 19 to 25.

➤   Majority (62.5%) of the respondents are graduates having monthly income less than Rs 30000.

The following findings are about the satisfaction level of

respondents towards online shopping behavior.

➢ Majority (39.5%) of the respondents have agreed that online shopping is convenient and time saving.

➢ Majority (39.25%) of the respondents agreed that they are price conscious customers.

➢ Majority (35.9%) of the respondents agreed that they are value conscious customers.

➢ Majority (38.33%) of the respondents agreed that online shopping is very useful and gives the ability to search for the products in a flash from the comfort of your home.

➢ Majority (37.2%) of the respondents have agreed that online shopping is available 24x7 Anytime Anywhere, and offers variety of choices, quick, better, and hassle free services.

➢ Majority (40.5%) of the respondents is neutral and they perceive that online shopping provides enjoyment and a fun filled experience.

➢ Majority (38.38%) of the respondents are neutral regarding the quality of service they get, while making purchases online.

➢ Majority (40.67%) of the respondents have agreed that the quality of the websites appeals more customers while buying.

➢ Majority (41.83%) of the respondents have agreed that better communications are made with the customers while shopping online.

➢ Majority (33.5%) of the respondents agreed that they are more concerned about the social risk involved in online shopping.

➢ Majority (33.67%) of the respondents have agreed that cases of delayed delivery, damaged or inferior goods, quality issues and even instances of cheating where the goods were never shipped was one such concern.

➢ Majority (39.83%) of the respondents have agreed that online shopping involves financial risk.

➢ Majority (37.25%) of the respondents have agreed that they are reluctant to use online shopping with a fear that their bank/ credit cards details might be stolen.

➢ Majority (33.5%) of the respondents are neutral regarding the product risk involved.

4.3 Suggestions of The Study

➢ Companies should have more risk reduction activities as perceived risk could strongly influence consumer's online purchase decisions. And specific types of perceived risk like online frauds should be taken care of in different scenarios. Hence, the shopping sites should sport a Certificate of Authenticity.

➢ Companies should improve consumer's value perceptions about the products and reduce consumer's perceived risk by providing quality products, timely delivery and fulfill their expectations. Also the companies should make their website easy in use and risk reduction activities should be taken care.

➢ The right to get correct weights and measures could be achieved based on standard measuring units so it helps to compare prices of different goods and materials in the unit that is specified.

<u>**Register Online**</u> with the National Consumer Helpline portal of Ministry of Consumer Affairs, Food and Public Distribution and file a complaint online. Check the status of previously filed complaints; all packaged items have to be labelled with information regarding weight, product name, and expiry.Raise a complaint with the Bureau of Indian Standards with regards to ISI marked products,file a complaint with the Internet Crime Complaint Centre (IC3) for internet-based crimes. If consumer rights are respected online shopping will become a way of life.

References

1. Bhatnagar, A., S. Misra, and H. R. Rao. 2000. "On Risk, Convenience, and Internet Shopping Behavior", *Communications of the ACM (Association for Computing Machinery)*, Vol. 43, No. 11: 98-105.

2. Bhattacharya et. al., 2004. The impact of quickness, price, payment risk and delivery issues on online shopping, *Journal of socio economics*, Vol.33, 2004, pp.241-251

3. Bourlakis, M., Papagiannidis, S. and Fox, H. 2008. "E-consumer behaviour: Past, present and future trajectories of an evolving retail revolution", *International Journal of E-Business Research,* Vol. 4, no.

3, pp.64-67, 69, 71-76.

4.	Butler,	P. and Peppard, J.1998. "Consumer purchasing on the internet: Processes and prospects", *European Management Journal,* Vol. 16, no. 5, pp.600-610.

5.	Curtis,	J. 2000. Cars set for online sales boom. Marketing, 10 Feb, pp. 22 – 23.

6.	Dan, Y., Taihai, D., and Ruiming, L. 2007. "Study of Types, Resources and Their Influential Factors of Perceived Risks in Purchase Online", *Journal of Dalian University of Technology*, 28 (2), 13-19.

7.	Delafrooz, N, Paim L.H., Haron, S.A., Sidin, S.M., Khatibi, A. 2009. Factors affecting students' attitude toward online shopping.*Afr. J. Bus.Manag.*, 3(5):200-9.

8.	Eggert, A. 2006. "Intangibility and Perceived Risk in Online Environments", *Journal of Marketing Management*, Vol. 22, No. 5/6: 553-572,

9.	Forsythe, S.M. and B. Shi. 2003. "Consumer Patronage and Risk Perceptions in Internet Shopping", *Journal of Business Research*, Vol. 56: 867-875,

10.	Garbarino,E. and M. Strahilevitz. 2004. "Gender Differences in the Perceived Risk of Buying Online and the Effects of Receiving a Site Recommendation", *Journal of Business Research*, Vol. 57: 768-775,.

11.	Horton, R. L. 1984. "The Structure of Perceived Risk: Some Further Progress", *Academy of Marketing Science*, Vol. 4, No. 4: 694-716,

12. Jacoby, J. and L. B. Kaplan, "The Components of Perceived Risk", in Venkatesan, M. (Ed.), Proceedings of the Third Annual Conference, Association for Consumer Research, Iowa City, Iowa, pp. 382–393, 1972.

13. Jun, Guo. And Noor, Ismawati Jaafar. 2011. Study on Consumers' Attitude towards Online Shopping in China International. *Journal of Business and Social Science*, Vol. 2 No. 22; 125.

14. Keeney, R.L.1999. "The value of internet commerce to the customer", *Management Science*, vol. 45, no. 4, pp. 533-542.

15. Lee, Younghwa. Kozar, Kenneth, A. and Larsen, Kai, R.T. 2003. "The Technology Acceptance Model:Past, Present, and Future". *Communications of the Association for Information Systems*: Vol.12, Article 50.

16. Lim, H. and Dubinsky, A.J. 2004. "Consumers' perceptions of e-shopping characteristics: An expectancy-value approach", *The Journal of Services Marketing*, Vol. 18, no. 6, pp.500-513.

17. Lu, H.P., C.L. Hsu, and H.Y. Hsu. 2005. "An Empirical Study of the Effect of Perceived Risk upon Intention to Use Online Applications", *Information Management & Computer Security*, Vol. 13, No. 2/3: 106-120.

18. Nagra, G., and Gopal, R. 2013. A study of Factors Affecting on Online Shopping Behavior of Consumers. *International Journal of Scientific and Research Publications*, Vol. 3, No. 6, pp. 1- 4.

19. Peter, J.P. and L.X. Tarpey. 1975. "A Comprehensive

Analysis of Three Consumer Decision Strategies", *Journal of Consumer Research*, Vol. 2: 29-37.

20. Tech, Faq. 2008. "Top reasons why people shop online," http://www.thetechfaq. Com/2008/09/29/top-reasons-why-people-shop-online/, hetechfaq.com

21. Wang, C.L., Ye, L.R., Zhang, Y. and Nguyen, D.D. 2005. "Subscription to fee-based online services: What makes consumer pay for online content*Journal of Electronic Commerce Research*, Vol. 6, no. 4, pp.301-311.

22. Yu, T. Wu, G. 2007. "Determinants of internet shopping behavior: An application of reasoned behavior theory", *International Journal of Management*, Vol.24, no. 4, pp.744-762, 823.

CHAPTER
18

ROLE OF INDIAN POLICE AND HUMAN RIGHTS

Mrs. Poonam Dutta
Associate Professor
Department of Political Science
Govt. College, Sri Karanpur
Sri Ganganagar
(Rajasthan)

Dr. Sanjeev Kumar Bansal
Associate Professor Department of ABST
SNDB Govt. P.G. College,
Nohar- Hanumangarh
(Rajasthan)

Dr. Navneet Verma
Associate Professor
Department of Hindi
Ch. Ballu Ram Godara Govt. Girls College,
Sri Ganganagar
(Rajasthan)

Introduction

Human Rights in India is an issue complicated by the country's large size and population, and its diverse culture, even though being the world's largest sovereign, secular, democratic republic. Human Rights are those rights that are fundamental for the human life.These rights are inherent to every individual and for this season it is called Human Rights. Human Rights are very much essential for a good and qualitative human survival liberty of the individual and respect for his dignity. These rights are fundamental to every human being but still there are several occurrences of human rights violations in India which creat a need for some authority to regulate such issues.

The violation of human rights has become a common phenomenon in the recent times. One can come across the human rights violation cases almost everybody throughout the political landscape of the world. It is ironic to see that whereas the state is the guarantor and protector of human rights, Most of the cases are registered against the state itself, which concern the violence of human rights. Generally Human Rights violations committed by police. In India the image of the police of Public mind is not much different from that in the British Period, when it was used to suppress the people with an iron hand. People still perceive the police as brutal, corrupt and inefficient. In fact the police have shown all the three faces, i.e., as a savior, a victim and an abusing force, in the domain of human rights violations in our country. The observance of human rights by the police has already become mandatory by law and they have no choice in the matter. Any violence will invite legal action and punishment. This issue basically involves a question of values and ethics.

Role of Police in India

In a well-ordered democracy and welfare state the police is supposed to be a disciplined force trained to uphold the law and enforced democratic institution to function on constitution lines. In India the British colonial administration introduced a police system primarily to protect and defined the establishment. A sort of police raj did surely take shaped by 1947, where the police was a major player in the ordering of rural and urban society, in the suppression of political opposition and in consolidation of state control.

The Indian constitution, with the ideals of equality, liberty and social justice has brought a new perspective on the role of police in performance of their duties. The police in a democratic society is required to perform multifarious functions, besides the maintenance of law and order. It is the only agency that has the widest possible contact with the people. Police functions are mostly prohibitive and regulatory in nature and this leaves an impression on the individual citizens that police interferes with the life, liberty and freedom of the people. It is that public institution which widely affects large sections of population in their everyday lives, more seriously than any other agency of government. In fact, the role of police has been redefined to include the values of democratic polity, secularism, social justice, human dignity and building up a democratic image of police to serve the community.

Human Rights Violations by the Police

The Human Rights violations committed by the police take several forms, beginning with illegal detention/arrest, false implications, use of torture that may lead sometimes to deaths in custody. The police are permitted to use force under certain circumstances mainly in case of arrest and search. The police are also permitted to use civil force for dispersal of an unlawful assembly and if necessary by arresting and confining those involved. The police are frequently criticised for use of excessive force during interrogation in police custody. Police image in the estimate of public has badly suffered by the prevalence of this practice in varying degrees.

The Asian centre for Human Rights estimated that from 2002 to 2008, over four people per day died while in police custody, with 'hundreds of those deaths being due to police use of torture. According to a report written by the institute of correctional Administration in Punjab, up to 50% of Police officers in the country have used physical or mental abuse on prisoners. Instance of torture, such as through a lack of sanitation space or water have been documented in West Bengal as well. The number of deaths in police custody as reported to the NHRC has shown a decline in a number of states, with Bihar, Kerala, Orissa, M.P., Punjab, Rajasthan, Tamilnadu, Karnataka and Pondicherry. In India; an attempt has been made since 1999 to gather information on details of cases where human rights were violated due to Police excesses such as 'illegal Detentions; 'Fake Encounters', Extortion, 'Torture', etc. by National Crime Record Bureau, New Delhi and National Human Rights Commission, New Delhi, under home Ministry, Government of India. The details are presented by NCRB's crime in India report 2008, that as per the report 253 cases of Human Rights violation by police were reported throughout the country during 2008.

Whenever violations of human rights by police are reported it causes an overall effect of loss of faith in the police as a protector and upholder of citizens rights. The failure to respect human rights in every day, police process alienates public sympathy and support which leads to undermining the people's confidence in public.

Code of conduct for Police in India

The code of conduct for police in India is based on the principle of necessity and proportionality. The Ministry of Home Affairs developed the following principles as code of conduct for police in India.

1. The police must bear faithful allegiance to the constitution of India and respect and uphold the rights of the citizens as guaranted by it.

2. They should enforce the law firmly and impartially without fear or favour.

3. The Police should recognize and respect the limitations of their powers and functions.

4. The prime duty of the police is to prevent crime and disorder and the police must recognize that the test of their efficiency is the absence of both and not the visible evidence of police action in dealing with them.

5. They should always be ready to offer individual service and friendship.

6. The police should recognize that their full utility to the state is best ensured only by maintaining a high standard of discipline.

7. The police must recognize that they are members of the public with the only difference being that in the interests of society and on its behalf they are employed to give full attention to duties.

8. The police should always place duty before self, should remain calm in the face of danger and should be ready to sacrifice their lives in protecting those of others.

9. The police should always be courteous and well-mannered. They should be dependable and impartial. They should possess dignity and courage.

10. As members of a secular, democratic state, the police should strive continually to rise above personal prejudices and should promote harmony and the spirit of common brotherhood among all of the people of India.

Police Reforms

Since independence the need for through reforms has been felt and urged not only by civil society and academic observers but by the government itself. Recently once again the government has expressed its readiness to replace the archaic 1861 Police Act with a new law and to increase accountability and upgrade procedures to handle everybody crime. The NHRC has been doing commendable work in continuously encouraging the police forces of various states, through their high ranking officers, in spreading human rights education. The commission also organizes and supports various seminars aimed at making police personnel aware of the importance of human rights. NHRC favour of depoliticisation of the higher ranks of the police. It has suggested that frequent transfers of the state police chief should be discouraged, police should be made less authoritarian, Yet more accountable, and the investigated branch should be separated from the law and order handling, and thus it should be insulted extraneous pressures.

In fact policing essentially is a public service and in a democracy it is responsive to the people. It is that public institution which widely affects large sections of population in their everybody lives, more seriously than any other agency of government.

References

1.　Crawshaw, Crawshaw. Human Rights and Policing.

2.　Ghosh,S.K.Police and the Public.

3.　Kamminga, Menno T. Inter-State Accountability for Violations of Human Rights ,

4.　Mangali, R.N. A study of Human Rights violation by Police in India. *International Journal of Criminology and Sociological Theory,* Vol. 3

5.　Mishra, Sharad Chand. Police Administration in India.

6.　Naath, Trilok.The Police Problem.

7.　Prasanna, S.B.M. Role of Police in Protection of Human Rights.

8.　Prasanna. Role of Police in Protection of Human Rights. A Review by: Indian Social Science Journal.

CHAPTER
19

PROTECTION AND PROMOTION OF HUMAN RIGHTS IN INDIA : ROLE OF NATIONAL HUMAN RIGHTS COMMISSION

Dr. Girdhar Lal Sharma

Principal,

Syon College

Hanumangarh Road,

Abohar

(Punjab)

Introduction

Human rights are inherent, inalienable and fundamental rights to enjoy dignified life. Human beings are entitled to enjoy certain fundamental rights irrespective of any distinction of race, religion, caste, sex and place of birth, etc. The rights have acquired special status at global level owing to their ubiquitous availability. At international level, plethora of human rights, treaties, declarations and conventions have been formulated to furnish ample guidance to world's governments to bring their municipal laws in tune with global mandate to protect and promote human rights. The government of India has also given due recognition to several human rights in part three and part four of Indian Constitution. The part-III titled 'fundamental rights' and part-IV 'directive principles of state policy' incorporate several civil, political and economic rights respectively. Having inspired from Constitutional obligation to respect and promote human rights and in compliance of international mandate on human rights, the government of India passed specific The Protection of Human Rights Act in 1993 which aims to protect and promote human rights in India. Under the Act, Statutory body known as National Human Rights Commission has been set up to protect and promote human rights. Since the establishment of NHRC is going to complete its 25 years of working in area of protection of human rights, it would be desirable here to assess its performance. Therefore, the objective of the present paper is to assess working and performance of the NHRC to know whether it succeeded to accomplish the task assigned to it under the Act.

NHRC as Defender and Protector of Human Rights

Since its establishment the NHRC is dealing with multiple forms of human rights violations. It not only performed several activities to protect and promote human rights in India but at several occasions issued directions to governments and their instrumentalities to respect human Fights of vulnerable section of the society. The human rights of women, children, and prisoners, accused and under trials have been given special recognition. Under the following sub-heads the initiatives taken by NHRC in area of protection and promotion of human rights has been disused.'

a. Human Rights of Trafficked Women and Children

In India thousands of women and children are victims of human trafficking. They-are trafficked for several sexual and non-sexual based purposes 1 such as prostitution, commercial sexual exploitation, pornography, drug peddling, fraudulent marriages, and illegal transplantation of body parts, illegal adoptions and child and bonded labour, etc. The NHRC in such cases took suo motu actions and directed governments to rehabilitate them to prevent possibility of their relapsing into business of prostitution and commercial exploitation. The Commission stressed on rescue of women and children engaged in sexual and non sexual based activities. The NHRC pleaded for the abolition of the practice of bonded and child labour and issued several directions to governments to rehabilitate and resettle rescued children found working in tanneries and industries in various parts of the country. Special efforts have been made by the Commission to free the children from the bondage in state of Maharashtra, Punjab, Bihar, UP, MP and Jharkhand etc.

b. Human Rights of Schedule Caste and Schedule Tribes

Schedule castes and schedule tribes are the worst victims of socio-economic exploitation. Take for example, schedule tribes residing in forest areas are often displaced due to developmental projects which amounts violation of their various rights such as right to livelihood, right to live human dignity, right to life and personal liberty, right to education, right to family, right to property, cultural and customary rights and right to carry on any occupation and trade. But large infrastructure projects have resulted into their displacement. The NHRC in various cases of manmade, natural and conflicts induced displacements gave appropriate directions to governments' and project authorities to rehabilitate and resettle them.? The commission ensured that schedule tribes should be rehabilitated in compact block so that they can enjoy their special customs, traditions and usages. The committees of experts constituted by the Commission also visited to schedule tribe's hamlet to see the ground realties. The Commission recommended stern action against those who were found guilty of violating human rights of SC and discriminating in one or the other ground.

c. Human rights of Prisoners and Under trials

Prisoners accused and under trials are also entitled to enjoy several basic human rights. Like ordinary citizens, they are capable to enjoy human rights such as right against solitary confinement, right against custodial torture, inhuman and degrading treatment, and right to speedy trial, right to free legal aid, right not to be hanged in public place, right to write a book in jail and so many other basic rights.3 But it has been witnessed in India that many prisoners and under trials have become object of exploitation and injustice by custodial institutions. They have subjected to custodial torture, rapes, illegal arrest, detention and other forms of injustice. It is worthwhile to state here that in India custodial torture, harassment by police, custodial deaths, fake encounters, custodial rapes, illegal arrest and detention, inhuman and degrading treatment of prisoners and under trails have been common. The NHRC in several cases punished and fined erring and guilty police and jail authorities and officers involved in degrading and humiliating prisoners and under trials. The human rights violations by police have also been dealt with iron hands.

d. Human Rights violation by Other State Agencies

It is not only the custodial institutions which are found to be involved in violations of human rights of vulnerable but different other state agencies are also involved in human rights violations. In such cases, the NHRC also condemned actions of public officials. For example, in allegations of death, rape and torture of tribals by joint task force set up by the government of Tamil Nadu and Karnataka to apprehend Veerappan and associates had been dealt with seriously.4 The human rights violations cases by security forces such as BSF and other security forces deployed at border areas and in state of J &K have become common and in such cases NHRC recommended exemplary punishment and fine. The killing of two civilians by a BSF Jawan, In District Gangbanger, Rajasthan and death of Vikram by Negligence of RPF in Maharashtra has been some of the cases wherein one can see grave negligence on part of security forces.

e. Protection of Economic, Social and Cultural Rights

Besides above mentioned specific violation of human rights by State agencies and custodial institutions, the NHRC also took bold stand to protect human rights of disabled and HIWAIDs victims. The Commission paid great heed towards the protection of human rights of fetus, right to health and rights of women in case of sex tourism. The women victims of acid attack are entitled for several human rights.6 The Commission showed concern towards the plight of the victims of acid attacks and issued directions to the governments to do the needful for the welfare of the victims.

The NHRC emphasized on the need to rehabilitation of marginalized and destitute women in vrindavan. The Commission for the sake of protection and promotion of human rights did not hesitate to visit to mental hospital and other state institutions such as juvenile boards, homes, rain basaira and old age shelter homes, etc in order to monitor the role and approach of governments towards upholding the interests of such people.

f. Other initiatives taken by Commission to Protect and Promote Human Rights

Since its inception in 1993, the NHRC has undertaken several activities in area of protection and promotion of human rights? The Commission is continuously organizing workshops, seminars, campaigns, nukar natak to make people aware about human rights especially in slums and rural areas. Besides, it is conducting research studies and carrying out projects. It has completed several research projects and some of the projects and research is still going on. The studies which are still going on are on topic of varied nature such as implementation of the Juvenile justice care and protection, current trends in child labour in industries, feminization of poverty and impact of globalization and a study of the human rights status of de-notified and nomadic communities of Delhi, Gujarat and Maharashtra.

In addition, the Commission is incurring huge expenditure on publication of material on human right to make people aware about rights. It is organizing internships programmes for students of different colleges and universities from diverse parts of the country. International co-operation in area of protection of human rights has also been encouraged by the commission. The annual meetings, discussion and conferences with foreign delegates are common whereby the Commission is interacting with representatives of various countries on issues of terrorism, environment pollution problem, communicable diseases and trafficking of women and children. All such problems are trans-boundary in dimensions which also can be tackled with concerted efforts of the world community to prevent so called universal human rights violations.

Conclusion and Suggestions

The preceding discussion makes it amply dear that the Commission is doing wonderful job in area of protection and promotion of human rights. It is taking suo motu cognizance of the human rights violations and issuing directions to the states and their agencies to prevent violations. Likewise, it is frequently entraining human rights complaints from different parts of the country and did not scare from imposing penalties and fines on erring and guilty state agencies. The interests of vulnerable sections of the society such as women, children, and members of schedule caste, schedule tribes and old aged persons have been specifically safeguarded. During its more than two decades. Working, it has exhibited great role towards protection and defending human rights. The people have been frequently made aware about their human rights through modus of workshops, seminars, symposium and conferences. The regular expenditure on expansion of libraries and other infrastructure in the office of the Commission which is situated at Delhi clearly shows that the Commission is serious in taking and dealing human rights complaints. But despite of its good performance, there are certain hurdles in effective enforcement of human rights on part of the Commission. One of the major impediments is that the Commission is only a recommendatory body and it has no power to punish those persons who defy its orders. Moreover, the Commission has no powers to enforce and ensure the compliance of its orders. It lacks financial autonomy. These are some of the problems which need to be tackled at the earliest to make the Commission, a robust statutory body to enforce human rights of the vulnerable.

References

1.	Id., at 41.

2.	Kamaljeet and Verma, Harish. 2004. *"Trafficking of Women and Children in India: A Human Rights Perspective"*. 48 Panjab University Law Journal 256-66 (2004).

3.	National Human Rights Commission Annual Report (2004-2005).

4.	National Human Rights Commission Annual Reports (2001-2013).

5.	National Human Rights Commission Annual Reports (2008-2009).

6.	Sindu, Sanjay and Verma, Harish. 2003. *"Custodial Violence in India: A Historical Introspection"*. Journal of Guru Nanak Dev University Law Amritsar.

7.	The Indian Perspective, 48 Civil and Military Law Journal 197.207 (2012)

8. Verma, Harish. 2010. *"Illegal Kidney Trade in India: A Problem of Great Concern"*. 116 Cri.L.J 184.92.

9. Verma, Harish. 2012. *"Acid Violence against Women and its Sodo-Legal Implications: The Indian Perspective"*. 48 Civil and Military Law Journal 197. 207.

www.ingramcontent.com/pod-product-compliance
Lightning Source LLC
Chambersburg PA
CBHW051952150726
47999CB00004B/1350